# Gangs
# To
# Jobs

---

## FAITH-BASED GANG INTERVENTION
## FOR YOUR CITY

---

*by Rev. Roger Minassian*

Alpha Publishing, Inc.

Library of Congress Card Catalog Number 2003113268
ISBN   0-9717585-4-9

Grateful acknowledgment is made to the following for permission to reprint from copyrighted
material. All rights reserved.

1. *Why L.A. Happened: Implications of the '92 Los Angeles Rebellion*, edited by Haki R.
Madhubuti, Third World Press, Chicago, Copyright 1993 by Haki R. Madhubuti.

2. *Do or Die*, Leon Bing, Harper Perennial, New York, Copyright 1992 by Leon Bing.

3. *There Are No Children Here: The Story of Two Boys Growing Up in the Other America*, Alex
Kotlowitz, Anchor Books/Doubleday, New York, Copyright 1991 by Alex Kotlowitz.

4. *Fatherless America: Confronting Our Most Urgent Social Problem*, David Blankenhorn, Basic
Books, New York, Copyright 1995 by Institute for American Values.

5. *Strengthening Your Grip*, Charles R. Swindoll, W. Publishing Group, Nashville, Copyright
1982 by Charles R. Swindoll.

6. *Uprising: Crips and Bloods Tell the Story of America's Youth in the Crossfire*, Yusuf Jah and Sister
Shah'Keyah, Scribner (an imprint of Simon & Shuster Adult Publishing Group), New York,
Copyright 1995 by Yusuf Jah and Sister Shah'Keyah.

7. *FistStickKnifeGun*, Geoffrey Canada, Beacon Press, Boston, Copyright 1995 by Geoffrey
Canada.

8. *Too Young to Die: Bringing Hope to Gangs in the Hood*, Gordon McLean, Focus on the Family/
Tyndale House Publishers, Wheaton, Copyright 1998 by Gordon McLean.

9. *Peace in the Streets: Breaking the Cycle of Gang Violence*, Arturo Hernandez, CWLA Press,
Washington, Copyright 1998 by Child Welfare League of America, Inc.

Most Scriptures are taken from the Holy Bible, New International Version, Copyright 1973, 1978,
1984 International Bible Society, used by permission of Zondervan Bible Publishers. Other
Scriptures are taken from the Holy Bible, New Living Translation, Copyright 1996, used by
permission of Tyndale House Publishers, Inc., Wheaton, Illinois 60189. All rights reserved. The
language in some verses has been modified to increase gang youth understanding.

Hope Now youth-client names and certain details of the stories in this book have been changed to
protect the privacy of the individuals involved. However, the facts and the underlying principles
have been conveyed as accurately as possible.

Alpha Publishing, P.O. Box 53788, Lafayette, Louisiana 70505
Published in U.S.A.

# ✦ ———————————————— CONTENTS

Page

## PART ONE
### What God Did in Central California

## PART TWO
### What God Wants to Do in Your City

# Acknowledgments

If I knew how difficult it would be to write a book, I would never have started. By the grace of God, I found an interested publisher and that motivated me to become, as my wife put it, "a man possessed." Thank you Kathleen Dunham of Berean Christian Stores for enthusiastically pointing me to Alpha Publishing and publisher Mark Anthony, who believed in both the messenger and the message of this book.

My great debt of gratitude begins with the true founder of Hope Now For Youth, the Lord Jesus Christ. His was the idea revealed, His is the plan unfolding, and His is the splendor being shown. We have merely followed Jesus.

Without the perseverance, risk-taking, and uncommon dedication of the Hope Now staff, past and present, many of whom are named in the book, there would be no story to tell. And to each of the young men whose stories here will enliven hope on other streets, I know God smiles upon you.

I am particularly appreciative of my coworker, John Raymond, who reviewed the manuscript and suggested many helpful changes and additions. Yet the raw product of six months effort still would have been less understandable without the consummate editing abilities of my sister in Christ, Carol Dice.

Finally, to my wife Marilyn, my finest earthly joy and the most hard working volunteer for Hope Now, thanks for being my greatest encouragement and life companion. God bless you for following that 53-year-old dreamer into the streets ten years ago.

# Dedication

This book is dedicated to all the gang young men and their families who will yet find Life because you, the reader, followed the heavenly vision. To God be the glory.

# Part One
## *What God Did in Central California*

# CHAPTER 1

# A Fiery Wake-up Call

*Again and again, I informed white reporters that the
Black folks who were destroying property and looting
were not engaging in some aberrant behavior. That they
in fact were showing just how American they are, for
material goods and property are what we are socialized
to believe really matters, not human life or human well-
being.*

bell hooks
*Why L.A. Happened*

"Most of us here don't care about these kids as long as they
shoot each other." The fear and anger infecting this mother's
heart were paralyzing my city of 386,000 in 1992. Shocked by
gang ruthlessness as the major cause of 87 homicides, and terri-
fied of home invasions on dark streets, Fresno was in a freefall to
hopelessness. Night after night on the evening news and day after day in our newspaper, gang violence was killing our children.
Senseless arguments over turf or colors or drugs were erupting
into automatic weapon's fire crackling through neighborhoods.
Our police were outgunned and undermanned, so the calls for
law and order were impotent to effect change. California was
building prisons faster than ever, but not fast enough to make
our streets any safer.

With 14,400 vehicles stolen in 1992, Fresno had also earned
national notoriety as the car-theft capital of California, second
only to Newark, New Jersey in vehicles stolen per capita. So it
came as no surprise to Fresnans that our city was ranked No. 277
out of 277 in a national survey of desirable places to live. That
was the way we felt: ranking last was well deserved. From watch-

ing television and reading our only daily newspaper, the *Fresno Bee*, we had come to believe that our city was substandard and that gang members, who were either crazy or irretrievably evil, were a major cause. Why do they do these terrible things? Why can't the police control them? Where are their parents? What are the schools doing? Will my car be where I parked it? These questions kept demanding answers, but we didn't have any.

In response to this threatening storm of lawlessness, Rev. G. L. Johnson, pastor of our largest church, the Peoples Church, called his fellow ministers to a prayer retreat for our churches, our city, and ourselves in March of 1992. Forty of us gathered at the Episcopal Church and Conference Center outside the quaint mountain village of Oakhurst to pray for almost four days, ten hours a day. I had never prayed even one day for ten hours but, led by the Northwest Renewal Team, we sensed that God was doing something to break down the walls between the Christians of our city. What this had to do with renewing Fresno was yet to be seen.

I returned to pastoring my church, wondering what God had in mind for me, for us, for our city. Having spent the last 12 of my 22 years of parish ministry at Pilgrim Armenian Congregational Church, I felt I had done all God had gifted me to do in that situation. As for the future, all I knew was that I did not feel led to pursue another parish position. But God had more to tell me, and I didn't have long to wait before he spoke. On Thursday, April 30, 1992 I came home from conducting a women's retreat, oblivious to the destruction occurring 200 miles away. Like most Americans, I stared at my TV set in disbelief: Los Angeles was burning. In response to a verdict by a white jury that exonerated white policemen who beat Rodney King to the ground, South Central L. A. had exploded. The amateur video of the beating of this kneeling black man had been seen worldwide. Now this verdict had incited rage. Police cars were being overturned, convenience stores were being set on fire, and thousands were swarming in a frenzy of looting. As I watched hour after hour of this rebellion expanding beyond police control, I began to feel a gnawing sense of hopelessness. Don't these people have jobs to go to? Why are they setting fire to their only stores? Will this spread to the rest of LA? When and how will this end? Yet there was another more urgent question that incessantly hammered away at my dwindling comfort zone.

On Friday evening, I gathered with several friends from my church to pray for our own city, which was rumbling. All day Saturday, the looting and fires in Los Angeles continued, but the police were beginning to gain some control. By Sunday, the streets of South Central were simmering down to scenes of quiet devastation. Yet my heart was anything but quiet. God used that fiery wake-up call to ignite a passionate curiosity within me. Here was the question to which my Lord required, no, demanded an answer: *"What kind of despair makes people set fire to their own neighborhoods?"* I had never experienced such hopelessness, but obviously there were thousands of people who did. My journey from middle class pulpit to "the other America" had begun.

Even though I grew up in New York City and in my early teenage years lived on 105th Street and West End Avenue, the borderline between the Jewish and Puerto Rican neighborhoods of the 1950s, I knew nothing about gangs. Once a stabbing took place in front of our apartment building, but that was the only crime I can remember in the neighborhood. Another time I was chased by some Puerto Rican kids and hit in the back by the fastest one as he called me a "dirty Jew." Although my best friends were Jewish, it didn't matter to my assailant that I was an Armenian, whose ancestors formed the first Christian nation state on earth.

My dad was a rug merchant turned Presbyterian minister, and mom was primarily a homemaker. From my father, I gleaned organizational skills; his favorite saying was, "Let's get organized!" Though he never went to college, Dad was widely read and loved to discuss the impact of politics and religion on everyday life. The goal he set before my brother and me was simple: "Each generation must improve on the last." Even before he was ordained, Dad spent a lot of his time trying to improve the Armenian Evangelical Church of New York. He was gone to meetings more nights than any of us care to remember. Yet through his insights and devotion, I gained a love for the Church and a desire to seek justice in society.

Mom gave me the inestimable gift of unconditional love, even if I never improved, a gift given to her by her father who died before I was born. She escaped the burning of Smyrna, Turkey in 1922 to immigrate to the United States during the Turkish massacres of the Armenians. Not speaking a word of English, she and her sisters would gather friends by juggling stones in the schoolyard. From mom's stories about the old country and her family's struggles here, I began to have an enduring faith in God and an abiding compassion for the underdog. That compassion sometimes still annoys my wife, Marilyn. As a tennis player in awe of the artistic power of Andre Agassi, I also root for anybody who can come close to beating him. I believe that it's fine for her to cheer the champion, but it's better for me to encourage the challenger going up against all odds. Becoming your best is more exciting to me than maintaining your best.

The Lord Jesus Christ offered his best to me when I opened my will to his purposes and my heart to his love at the University of California at Los Angeles in 1958. My freshman year had been spent at Davidson College in North Carolina, and the next year and a half I had attended Fresno State University. When I arrived as a junior on the doorstep of Alpha Gamma Omega Fraternity at UCLA, rumor had it amongst these Christ-centered brothers that I didn't speak a word of English. It seems I was to be their latest missions project!

My three years benefiting from the richness of this Christian brotherhood, and the durability of the faith God produced therein, initiated and encouraged my Christian service. So grateful was I for Alpha Gamma Omega that I got involved over the years with helping to start several chapters, including one at California State University, Fresno in 1987. This was where in 1988 I met a several struggling students from at-risk backgrounds who had recently given their hearts to the Lord. Through the men of AGO I also was made aware of the inner city youth work of the Evangelical Association for the Promotion of Education in Camden, New Jersey started by Dr. Anthony Campolo.

One of the churches attended by AGO members was the Calvary Presbyterian Church located in a changing neighborhood. Serving this mostly older congregation was Pastor John DeSanto, who felt called by the Lord to start a youth group of neighborhood kids. A Coffee Cup Ministry was started to reach out to the continuation school located across the street. From the youth met there, and from what was learned from the Camden work, the Calvary Vocational Placement Program was begun one month before the Los Angeles riots. The basis of the program appeared to be unique: If you were going to form a youth group of street kids, you had to also prepare them for, and find them jobs. Otherwise, they would never leave the gang lifestyle, the only source of income they knew.

With the press of my normal pastoral duties, it wasn't until a hot August 13 that I was introduced to three gang members in the program. For the price of a pizza lunch, I began learning from Jose, Ricky and Pe about the other America. Pe is on our staff today and has taken over 175 other gang members off the streets of Fresno in the last six years. Ricky, last I heard, was in the United States Army. The one we've lost track of, 14-year-old Jose, was the most articulate. Slight in build and with angular features, Jose was intense, anything but cool. I had been warned not to ask direct questions, so as not to be threatening, but Jose eagerly gave direct answers. When I asked the group, "Why do people join gangs," Jose replied, "I and my friends joined a gang for spending money." He wanted money for a hamburger, a video or a T-shirt. Too young for a job, and with no allowance or money for doing extra chores, Jose didn't see any legitimate ways to earn it. To sell some drugs or steal a car stereo appeared to be the only way in his neighborhood for a poor 14-year-old to get some cash. "And everybody needs money to live," he said.

But where were his parents? Why didn't they help out? When I asked him about his mother, I was stunned to hear, "I don't know who my mother is. She lives somewhere here in Fresno, but I've never met her." Only later, brought home to me by the hepatitis death of his 39-year-old aunt, did I realize that Jose's mother preferred her drugs to her son. Drugs were his father's problem, too, Jose said: "He's been in and out of jail for drug possession and sales all of my life. In fact he's getting out from a one-year jail term tomorrow." When asked if his father had any work skills, Jose replied, "I don't know of any." Several months later I found out that Jose had had a stepmother who was raped and murdered by his uncle, who now is serving 25 years to life in state prison. Jose lived with his 70-year-old grandmother, who received welfare for caring for him.

As I drove away from this heart-stretching lunch, I began to pray and I began to cry. Not one to cry easily, I asked myself why I was choking on my tears. Jose's story and what little the others said were sad enough, but as I examined my feelings, that was not why I was crying. Instead I was surprised by rage. I was crying because I was furious. If I were raised in the "family" Jose was raised in, I would be so hurt, so angry that I would want to kill everyone in sight! What ordained that my soul should enter this world in a family of two people who loved me, stayed together, gave me hope and a future including graduate school, and taught me about Jesus and his love, and what ordained that Jose's soul should arrive in that hellhole devoid of all hope that he has to call a family?

I was angry and crying over the unfairness of it all. Thoughts of my mother's suffering by oppression and poverty and of my father's exhortations to improve this world flashed through my mind. Jesus' invitation to the children to come to him and his dire warning if we lead them astray were convicting me. From what I experienced at lunch, I knew that these kids don't stand a chance of coming to Jesus or even finding a meaningful life, unless someone gives it to them. Somebody has to do something! These young men have no decent role model of what it means to be a man and so go to the streets to learn from other abandoned and abused youth. It is the blind teaching the lame to see and the lame teaching the blind to walk. Most of all, I knew that my Jesus wouldn't just let them bump and stumble. Could I? These kids had helplessness and hopelessness written all over them. But Another had inspired hope among the destitute almost 3000 years ago.

As God had planned it, my devotional reading that August

had brought me to this passage from Isaiah the prophet:

> *The spirit of the sovereign Lord is upon me, for he has anointed me to preach good news to the poor. He has sent me to bind up the broken-hearted; to proclaim freedom for the captives and release from darkness for the prisoners. To proclaim the year of the Lord's favor and the day of vengeance of our God. To comfort all who mourn and provide for those who grieve in Zion. To bestow on them a crown of beauty instead of ashes, the oil of gladness instead of mourning, and a garment of praise instead of a spirit of despair. They shall be called oaks of righteousness, a planting of the Lord for the display of his splendor.*
>
> *Isaiah 61:1-3*

For the next two weeks, the Lord interrupted my sleep many times, always with these verses running through my mind. Meanwhile, as I joined him for prayer, Pastor DeSanto kept saying, "Roger, this thing needs a father." By early September of 1992 I knew that I was that father. Jesus was calling me to follow him into the streets of our city, for he was weeping over these lost gang youth even more than I was. He wanted them to find a good life and life eternal even more than I did. What was being done in one church could be done in other churches. The vision was clear —an idea in the mind of God for the transformation of gang youth had been revealed. All we needed to do was follow him into the streets. But how dangerous was that? Was that really a smart and safe thing to do?

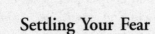 

# CHAPTER 2

## Settling Your Fear

*I'll be in a mall with a couple of the homies, and we'll be loked out in khakis and shades and stuff, and we'll see some church people there... To me they should be lookin' for the so-called sinner instead of the clean-cut one, probably already a Christian. I tell preachers this all the time, 'cause when they see us, they quick look the other way. I ask 'em, "Isn't Christianity about saving souls? Or are you only lookin' for people who already converted?" I ask 'em if they such strong Christians, why they so afraid of us? It ain't like gangbangers is the lions in this coliseum.*

*Do or Die, "Rider"*

If newspaper headlines and television news reports are the only source of what you know about gang members, it's easy to be fearful. If you or a friend had a home burglarized or a car stolen, it's natural to be deeply afraid. To be robbed and threatened at gunpoint can instill terror. This fear, assaulting you time and again but finding no constructive outlet, will inflame anger. In turn anger erects prisons, expensive rage-factories, monuments to our despair. Someday, almost all of those incarcerated will come out of prison, and return to our streets more angry, hopeless and desperate than ever. It is estimated that forty percent of all prisoners in our nation are being released in 2002.

The cycle of anger and fear had to be broken somewhere. When it came to a choice between me and a gang member, I decided that I was the least damaged. Fortunately, I had never been shot at, terrorized by a robber, or traumatized by a burglary of my home. Several times our car windows had been smashed and auto stereos stolen, usually during the night and in front of our home. But those events only made me more determined to do something. Any change in the status quo had to begin with me. First, I had to get over my own ignorance. I knew nothing about gang members, about why they acted the way they did. At my local Christian bookstore in 1992, I could find no books about gangs or Christians helping gangs. All I could find was *Nobody's Children* by Valerie Bell. Even searching today's Internet, I find very few books about Christians helping gang members.

Valerie Bell was a stay-at-home mom in a neighborhood of latchkey children, the subject of her book. Here was a gentle introduction to the world of abandoned and abused children, from which this challenge was imprinted on my heart:" We *are on the brink of a major societal tragedy if good people continue to be concerned only for their own flesh and blood children!"* God never allowed me to be concerned solely for my own flesh and blood children, because my wife and I couldn't give birth to any. Grieving through too many miscarriages made us think about all the other children who were already born, but didn't have parents to rear them. Since adopting our first child in 1968, the idea of taking care of somebody else's child has never been unusual to us. Two children came to us as infants and one at age 15. From Bell's statement, I was challenged to find out what *good* people, ordinary people like you and me, could *do* to help other people's children.

The second book I read about at-risk children was *There Are No Children Here: The Story of Two Boys Growing Up in the Other America* by Alex Kotlowitz. Locked in the violent vortex of the Henry Horner Homes, a public housing project in Chicago, Pharoah and Lafeyette Rivers are chronicled through two years of their desperate preteen lives. Kotlowitz writes:

> *…despite the youthful attire, he looked like an old man. There seemed bottled up in him a lifetime's worth of horrors. His face revealed a restless loneliness… And then I asked Lafeyette what he wanted to be. "If I grow up, I'd like to be a bus driver," he told me. If, not when. At the age of ten, Lafeyette wasn't sure he'd make it to adulthood.*

As I carefully and reflectively read through this very disturbing book, I began to comprehend the terror-filled childhoods that might inspire the hopeless desperation of gang violence.

Maybe you've heard the expression, "being dissed," in stories about gang violence. Gang members can be disrespected by a look, a color, a word, a hand sign, an enemy on their turf, graffiti, and a host of imagined or real slights. Every "dis" taps into the rage accumulated over years of having the vulnerabilities of childhood viciously violated. So you become hardened to keep from being hurt anymore. Your "rep" as a tough dude is important for survival on the streets. You don't want the reputation of being weak or a snitch. Inspiring fear, which gang members mistakenly equate with respect and manhood, is your best protection. A quick and violent temper can save your life. The more I understood the source of their rage, the less fearful and more compassionate I became.

The next critical part of my education was seeing a PBS documentary by Bill Moyers about the California Youth Authority entitled, *What Can We Do About Violence?* Listening to these incarcerated young men and women, I began to understand the causes of violence, the poisoned wells from which it is drawn. The hurts they described included growing up in a violent neighborhood and family, where divorce or unwed pregnancies led to fatherlessness and a lack of adult supervision. Some endured sexual abuse, others, physical abuse. Racism, drugs, and guns contributed to violence as a way of life. Parents and teachers gave up on them. While family and school were arenas for failure, they discovered they could never fail at crime.

Most riveting in this documentary were the comments of a young woman who was reflecting on how she got involved in violent crime: "How could a person get to the point where I didn't care, where I let myself be involved in torturing a man?"

"What's the answer to that?" Moyers asked.

Through tears she replied, "I think because I didn't have anyone care about me. I didn't think that I was good, so since nobody showed me I was important, I didn't have self-esteem.

I didn't care about anyone else. I wanted everyone to be as low as I was."

The message was clear. If you want me to care about others, I have to care about myself. And the only way I can learn to care about myself and think I'm important is if someone important cares about me and places value on me.

All these youthful felons found in their gang the acceptance and praise they never received at home, and they called it love. Their first experience of love was the camaraderie enjoyed with their neighborhood gang buddies (homies) while committing crimes, hanging out or partying. Sex was used for pain relief. Homies have rarely seen affection or caring without sex, so they can give very little of it even with sex. If there was one major deficit in their upbringing that is the root of all the anger, it was an almost total lack of caring from responsible adults. When you are five years old and watch your dad overdose on heroin in the bathtub, and then see your destitute mother turn to prostitution in your home, how much caring do you receive? What worth and value do you experience?

It began to dawn on me that caring is not a characteristic within us at birth, but is instilled by others who care. Parents, a grandmother, pastors and teachers cared for me, so I care about myself and others, and believe I am of value and worthy of a good future. Unless a child has received sufficient caring from responsible adults, he grows up not caring about himself and believes that he is of such little worth that no good future awaits him. He doesn't even care about his own property, what little there may be of it. Gang youth staying with friends often leave clothing and CD's when they move on. So if he doesn't care about his own life or property, why should he care about yours? If he believes his future is prison or death, why should yours be any better? With no hope for the future, with nothing to lose, why not commit desperate acts that inspire fear, demonstrate manhood and get "respect?" As I began to understand what creates gang crime and violence, compassion overwhelmed my fears. Later, however, I discovered that the streets of fear are open to two-way traffic.

The gang member fears our world as much as you may fear his. When Hope Now first started, I invited Alex and Noy to a Black Angus restaurant for dinner. I waited in the lobby and Alex finally came, but not Noy. After a while we took a table, but I kept looking for Noy. When we ordered, Alex asked for the same medium rare steak I did. Years later he told me that the only food he had ever ordered was fast and off a wall. Alex had never seen a menu so he ordered what I did, and he just played with the steak because "it looked like it was still alive." As for Noy, he said he had circled the parking lot of the restaurant for 15 minutes, looking for my car. Since I had parked in an adjacent lot, he couldn't find it. He left because it was just too scary for him to walk into that restaurant, his first restaurant, unless he was sure I was there. And these are the youth who handle guns like we handle salad forks. Each year at our Annual Banquet at the Radisson Hotel, we have to station staff outside the entrance to make sure former drive-by shooters have the courage to walk into a room that holds 900 people.

Homeowners who offer our youth odd jobs have to deal with fear also. Some are courageous enough to ask, "When they see all the nice stuff I have, won't they come back and steal it?"

"There are 1000 homes between where you live and they live," I reply as patiently as possible. "If they are going to continue to steal, yours is the last home they would choose because they know you are trying to help them by paying them for this odd job."

Some gang members are able to express gratefulness and may even momentarily give up that angry look to grant you a smile when you pay them. Our experience has shown that if a gang member is always smiling, he probably carries a lot of pain he no longer feels. Being a gang member does not produce happiness. So don't be deceived by the smiling mask or afraid of the "mad dog" look. Certainly in groups of their homies gang members can be pretty frightening, and even dangerous.

In front of each other on the streets, they strut and claw to achieve a perverse image of manhood. But I have yet to meet a gang member by himself who was anything but a hurting little child in an adult body eager for someone to listen and to care.

Probably because I have not been placed in great danger, my response to threat is more anger than fear. I don't skydive, hang glide or, as one of my more daring sons does, dive off rocks into mountain pools. However, in 1963 I did serve as Electronic Warfare Officer aboard an attack carrier 50 miles off the coast of Vietnam, but that's the closest I came to a war zone. When Muslim terrorists struck the World Trade Center and Pentagon, upending my niece's September 15, 2001 wedding, I couldn't wait to get on an airplane. When the anthrax scare hit our nation's capital, I couldn't wait to go there for her wedding. And on November 11 we did just that, our flights bracketing the Airbus crash on Long Island. As I searched the Scriptures during that awful time, God was telling me that the only safe place to be is in the will and doing the will of God. As I wrote to our Hope Now supporters, "The faithful Christian will fear God more than any terrorist threat, repent of not believing heaven is better, and continue doing God's will."

*"Don't be afraid of those who kill the body but cannot kill the soul. Rather, be afraid of the One who can destroy both soul and body in hell,"* Jesus said (Matthew 10:28). Fear can produce feelings of helplessness and hopelessness. It's one thing to suffer helplessness and hopelessness before the God of all help and hope, and wholly another to be overwhelmed by gang violence. If there is hopelessness greater than that in gang members, it is the hopelessness our society often feels toward gang members. Following our 1998 banquet, a judge called and said, "Until your banquet, I had absolutely no hope for gang kids." That sort of hopelessness used to be mine in early 1992. If I were going to continue on this journey of following Jesus to the streets, I realized that I needed to arrange my fears in the right order. From the three gang members I had met so

far, I concluded there was little to fear. Certainly in other set-
tings each of them had done violent and criminal acts. But
these were not "crazy or irretrievably evil" young men, as I
had thought. Here were hopeless, confused and frustrated
children who didn't know which way or to whom to turn.
When I told my wife their stories, she likewise saw little to
fear except my being unfaithful to the call growing in power
within me. Jesus was leading the way; I had to follow.

# CHAPTER 3

# Jesus Is Up Ahead

*Whoever welcomes one of these little children in my name welcomes me; and whoever welcomes me does not welcome me but the one who sent me.* Jesus

Mark 9:37

From the beginning, it was obvious that Jesus was up ahead saying, "Follow me." He wept over these young men more than I did. He was not afraid of them, had not abandoned them and had revealed a plan for them. One of the first verses that I came across after God used Isaiah 61:1-3 to call me was Psalm 68:5: *"A father to the fatherless, a defender of widows (single mothers), is God in his holy dwelling."* If I were going to follow God, then I too would have to become a father to the fatherless, a protector of single mothers struggling to raise sons with no man around. A few times I have wondered, "Why me?" But even when faced with calamity, my mother taught me to ask, "Why not me?" And here was an opportunity to do something good about a great calamity.

I've always loved something new to see or do. The thought of buying a mountain cabin or beach house and going to the same place all the time for vacation depresses me. Maintaining an organization that doesn't grow or attempt a new program drains the excitement out of my life. By previously implementing a counseling center at one church and a tutoring program at another, I became energized to do what was required each and every week to keep things running. Adding a new staff member and investing myself in their spiritual and personal development has usually been very fulfilling.

As I left Pilgrim Armenian Congregational Church to begin Hope Now, plans were underway for building the Harry and Zabelle Goorabian Family Life Center to minister to church and community youth. The idea for this facility gripped Zabelle Goorabian's heart during a Mother's Day sermon I preached the week after the 1992 Los Angeles uprising. Here was a lavish Christian response to the needs of the poor, needs deeply impressed upon us but one week earlier. Now that was exciting! Doubling or tripling a church's mission budget for the less fortunate was also a thrill. If a camel is a horse designed by a committee, these fresh accomplishments made up for a whole month of meetings designing camels that can never be ridden. Implementing these visions fulfilled my deep desire to show gratitude to my Lord, by remembering the poor he never forgot.

For far too long, middle class Christianity has tended to spiritualize what the Bible says about our responsibility to the poor. We have acted as if every mention of the poor means "poor in spirit," which Jesus mentioned only once. Every other allusion in Scripture to the poor means dirt poor, under our feet and despised, hungry and cold, disheveled and ignored poor. When we read that *"The Lord works righteousness and justice for all the oppressed,"* (Psalm 103:6) we bless Him and don't even think he wants to do it through us. If *"I know that the Lord secures justice for the poor and upholds the cause of the needy"* (Psalm 140:12), then that is part of my Christian duty if I am going to be like my Lord. I challenge everyone who has enough compassion to read this book to conduct a Bible concordance study on the occurrence of the words *poor, fatherless, justice, needy, oppressed,* and *widow.* A quick glance at Strong's Exhaustive Concordance of the Bible gave me 487 references. Meditate on what God says about your responsibility to the poor. It could be life-changing. Plan a time when you will start this now. To further make this point with our staff and board, I added a belief to our Statement of Faith that I have not found in any confession of faith: "I believe that material abundance is a trust from the Lord, and that God wills to meet the needs of the poor through the generosity of His people." Most of our street staff have come from lives of poverty, but even they need to learn to apply this truth.

It's easy not to see the poor. We live in two different worlds, separated by geography. Some Fresnans talk about not driving south of Shaw Avenue, because that's where many of the poor live, and where there is more crime. I too bought a house up north in 1980 when I became pastor of Pilgrim Armenian Congregational Church. For over 11 years it was easy to drive the freeway over poor neighborhoods without seeing people in need. Now I know what I was missing. The poor know they need hope and help; the more prosperous often do not. The poor are gifted and talented, but many times have had no legitimate opportunity to exercise those abilities.

Gratitude is a gift some of the poor can teach the rest of us. My wife and I were manning a Salvation Army kettle at Christmas, 2001 when one of our Hope Now youth, Sak, came through the mall with his little girl. After visiting a while, he put two dollars in the kettle, which was among the more generous of gifts during our volunteer shift. His was the gratefulness of the widow's mite. In 1996, Sak was a gangbanger without hope or a future. In his first placement, he worked for over a year as a houseman for Piccadilly Inn Airport hotel, and since 1997 Sak has been employed by Valley Children's Hospital. Where once he was a threat to human life, Sak today holds the lives of hundreds of children in his hands as a technician responsible for sterilizing surgical instruments and incubators. He plans to marry the mother of his children, who also works at the hospital as a pharmacy technician. Sak has a lot for which to be grateful.

Jesus pointed us to gratitude in the Parable of the Rich Fool. This wealthy farmer had so much prosperity that he didn't know what to do with it, so he devised bigger and better ways to hoard it. I rode with a rancher one day, mesmerized by his Cadillac's ability to register on the dash how many cylinders were being used to propel the car, from 4 to 6 to 8 and back again. He told me how he had just sold property for

$1,200,000 that cost him $300,000. In the next breath, just in case this pastor should get any crazy ideas about expecting financial generosity, the rancher stated that he needed all this to prepare for the *next great depression!* I didn't tell him that the next great depression was mine, over his lack of gratitude to God or concern for the poor. Hear our Lord clearly, *"A man's life does not consist in the abundance of his possessions… 'You fool, this night you will answer to God for your life. Then, who will get all that you have accumulated for yourself?' This is how it will be with anyone who stores up things for himself but is not rich towards God"* (Luke 12:15-21). And how can you be rich toward God? Our Lord taught that if we help the least of humanity, we have helped him.

The final result of all that I had experienced was the founding of Hope Now For Youth on February 1, 1993. I had been working what seemed like two full-time jobs since the previous September when I sent a letter to my congregation informing them of what God had shown us. If I had been smart, I would have given myself some space between leaving Pilgrim Armenian Congregational Church on Friday and starting Hope Now on Monday. But what I lacked in forethought I made up for in enthusiasm.

As I have followed Jesus on the streets of the city, he has shown me such depth of love that I was inspired to pen these words:

## THE LIGHTS ON THE PAVEMENT

I walk the long and dark,
Through alley, street and lurking park.
Who is that up ahead, or behind?
Is it so black or am I blind?

I see the shadows that were men,
Dead alive in their ghetto pen
Who might have found the unknown cure,
These wasted, who but now endure.

I hear the groans and awful sobs,
Pass the preening corner mobs.
Who waits there by that gloomy light
And fills my heart with surging fright?

I smell the dope that drains the soul,
And broken pieces makes of whole.
Who drowse in want of how to cope,
Outside the door, beyond the hope?

I taste the bitterness of wild despair,
The poison dregs that know no care.
Who else is at this empty feast,
This table of the very least?

I feel the hurt of hearts asunder,
The heavy roll of heaven's thunder.
Who am I to know both calls,
To open doors and break down walls?

I see it now, just a flash,
On that street strewn with trash.
Who has been this way before?
Who went past that much-locked door?

I hear a cry above the others,
And glimpse a spot, and then another.
Who in this grayness now appears?
Who fills my heart and drains my fears?

I smell the fragrance of love released,
Of harbor found, of hope increased.
Who makes this concrete desert bloom,
Splashing life, drowning doom?

I taste the sweetness of lavish care,
Glowing in circles of those who dare.
Who hosts this richest banquet time
Of friends who help the weak to climb?

I feel the drops of my own grief
Offered to God for their relief.
Who walks, sees, feels and hears,
Has marked the way with His own tears.

If you choose to have eyes to see, it's easy to see Jesus walking the streets of your city. Every once in a while he looks over his shoulder to see whether anyone is following. Can a wealthy businessman follow him into the streets? Yes, through marshalling financial and employment assets. Can an elderly woman follow him into the streets? Yes, through praying for gang youth. Can you follow him into the streets? Yes, through bringing God's resources to bear upon human need. Can an ex-gangbanger who now knows the Lord follow Jesus into those neighborhoods? Yes, if those prayers and resources are made available to support his ministry to transform lives. Open your Bible and open your newspaper; see if that is Jesus walking up ahead of you into the hopeless streets of gang members.

# CHAPTER 4

# The Other America

*There are exceptions, of course, but here is the rule: Boys raised by traditionally masculine fathers generally do not commit crimes. Fatherless boys commit crimes...*

*When the boy cannot separate from the mother, cannot become the son of his father, one main result, in clinical terms, is rage. Rage against the mother, against women, against society.*

David Blankenhorn
*Fatherless America*

In my reading through the Bible during the year, I found this passage that could well describe gang members.

*Listen, my child, to what your father teaches you.*

*Don't neglect your mother's teaching.*

*What you learn from them will crown you with grace*

*And clothe you with honor.*

*My child, if sinners entice you, turn your back on them!*

*They may say, "Come and join us. Let's hide and kill someone!*

*Let's ambush the innocent! Let's swallow them alive as the grave swallows its victims.*

*Though they are in the prime of life, they will go down into the pit of death.*

*And the loot we'll get! We'll fill our houses with all kinds of things!*

*Come on, throw in your lot with us: we'll split our loot with you."*

*Don't go along with them, my child! Stay far away from*

> *their paths.*
>
> *They rush to commit crimes. They hurry to commit murder.*
>
> *When a bird sees a trap being set, it stays away. But not these people!*
>
> *They set an ambush for themselves; they booby trap their own lives!*
>
> *Such is the fate of those who pursue illegal gain. It ends up robbing them of life.*
>
> Proverbs 1:8-19

But what happens when *you* are the one who is being neglected? Do you listen to your father or, more likely, your mother's boyfriend when he teaches you to steal cars? Should you heed your mother's teaching on how to shoplift and do drugs? What you learn from them will crown you with *dis*grace and clothe you with *dis*honor. If you neglect their teaching, as well you should, whom do you listen to?

The story is told about young male elephants on the edges of a game preserve that were threatening the surrounding farms and communities. They would trample fields by day and rampage through villages at night. As these adolescent bulls were also wounding each other in seemingly endless fights, they were being considered for extermination. Then one of the wardens observed that these young elephants had been moved to this new preserve and were growing up without any adult bulls around. "What would happen if we put an adult bull elephant in their midst?" he asked. As you can guess, soon after the adult male arrived, the juveniles were calmed down and began behaving more like the adult bull. Someone was in charge that they respected.

I wish I could tell you that young male humans act differently, but they don't. Fatherlessness is a common characteristic among families of young men who turn to gangs. An immigrant father who is not acculturated may be just as absent to an Americanized teenager as no father at all. Researchers who analyzed 11,000 separate crimes committed in three different urban areas concluded there was no clear link between crime and poverty or between crime and race. There was, how-ever, a strong correlation with "father-absent households." This finding doesn't mean that all or even most single mothers will raise delinquent sons. But when boys do become delinquent, it was found that a disproportionately high number of them live in fatherless homes.

In November of 1993 "60 Minutes" interviewed a brutal, cruel death-dealing gangbanger at Pelican Bay State Prison. The critical moment, missed by the interviewer, was when this buff, tough man spoke about his father. "Absent! Absent! Absent! I hate him! I hate him!" he cried as he lifted manacled hands to wipe the tears on his shirtsleeve. Intuitively, he felt that the pain he had suffered and the imprisonment he was enduring were somehow related to the father he never knew. In Hope Now caring means being the helpful father or the good older brother a youth never knew.

Prison Fellowship reported on a maximum-security peni-tentiary where Hallmark Cards offered free Mother's Day cards. The response was so overwhelming, the company made the same offer for Father's Day. *Not one prisoner requested a card!* Without the protection of a loving father, many had become prey for pedophiles. Some had even been shot or sexually molested by their own fathers. Most never got to know their fathers and had suffered abuse at the hands of other men.

When boys grow up without a positive male role model of a husband and a father, they have no idea of what a man is supposed to be. Gilbert's father walked off when he was two years old. Jose's father was a drunkard who abused his mother. Pao's father beat him bloody and never expressed any emotion except rage. How are these boys supposed to know what a man is? When Anthony's father disciplined him by shooting the little boy's dog, when Daniel's father threw his mother against the wall, when Isaac's father beat him with TV cables and chains, all these boys learn is what kind of father they *don't* want to be. Without intervention, however, they too will become raging and abusive fathers.

The Other America is one in which real men are absent. A

former Chicago Black Gangster Disciple told me that in his apartment project, there were *fathers without sons and sons without fathers.* Among the thousands who lived in his building, he knew of only one father living with his sons. One of our single Vocational Placement Counselors, Quion Calip, took Calvin to church with him on Father's Day. When all the fathers were asked to stand up, Calvin told Quion to stand up. When Quion protested, Calvin replied, "You can be my father." Tragically, unfathered young men, like elephants, often learn little or no impulse control and can become violent.

Many times the primary impulse is one of survival. Elvis, with no family worthy of the name, had to live with a cousin who has had five children by five different men. Spending her welfare money for drugs, she let her children go hungry. Elvis could earn the right to stay there by bringing home some food, any way possible. For showers he had to go to his aunt's overcrowded house because his cousin's bathtub was "full of bodies." To keep the large cockroaches from falling into his mouth while he slept, he put a sheet over his head. The refrigerator was usually empty, and so were their stomachs. The only way Elvis knew to get some money for food was to join with other poor neighborhood kids and sell some drugs, or steal a car stereo and fence it. In his mind the choice was "survive or die," and Elvis will always choose to survive. And in the other America, survival can become a full-time occupation.

When an eight-year-old death camp survivor was asked by an American Army rabbi, "How old are you?" he replied, "Older than you."

The rabbi had to laugh but the child told him, "Look, you cry and laugh like a little boy, but I haven't laughed for years and I don't cry any more. So tell me: who is older?"

Too many gang youth are older than we are. They don't know how to laugh or they laugh inappropriately when someone else suffers misfortune. Neither do they know how to play games. The horrors endured have made life far too serious. With so much to cry about, they don't cry. Many are angry because they never had the opportunity to be children, to be carefree and enjoy school. All they have known is this: "I'm a 13-year-old gang member and my friend who is 12 just had a baby. I've been to ten funerals in the past year and lost about two dozen friends, all under 20 years of age, but the violence keeps on happening." When your mother tells you that you will end up in prison like your loser father, and then abandons you, or your father hits you with fists, belts and boards while saying he wished you weren't his son, unimaginable wounds are knifed into your heart.

Who can think about the Pythagorean theorem when your stomach is growling and you are wondering who will jump you after school or where you will spend the night? School quickly becomes a babbling brook of irrelevant information flowing into the stream of your failures. You're late because nobody gets you up on time and later on you cut classes and run with your friends because they are going through the same "stress" you are. Your stepfather thinks everything is stupid except helping him do manual labor. Your crack-addicted mother gambles away $2000 of drug and welfare money, and runs around the apartment naked. You're so traumatized that you sleep in parks and doorways all over the city. No one at home cares, and certainly not about how you're doing at school.

Since you don't have the self-discipline to learn from a teacher because worries over life problems are overwhelming any academic thoughts, and since your life problems make you angry enough to start fights, they put you on "Home Study." Now you're supposed to take the work, do it at home and report once a week for two hours on your progress. What you couldn't do under the discipline of a teacher you are supposed to be able to do on your own. Home Study only erects another monument to failure in your life. But you know one area of life where you can never fail – you can always succeed at crime.

The business license to steal or to sell in your neighborhood, and in most poor neighborhoods, is held by the local crew, set or gang. These are the friends you grew up with, went to school with and cut classes with. The self-employed usually die. You need someone watching your back, like when another drug dealer horns in on your turf. And you want someone to party with when you get some "bread," or to fight alongside you when a rival gang insults your girl or disrespects your manhood.

Since gang members have rarely received genuine respect, which values and unifies, they substitute instilling fear, which demeans and divides. Respect is really important, particularly if you've never received the real thing. Whether it's called "significance," "worth" or "self-esteem," it is the need to know that someone cares about your well being, or at least if you are alive or dead. The lack of such caring results in the Characteristics of Gang Youth listed in the following table.

## CHARACTERISTICS OF GANG YOUTH

1. <u>HOPELESSNESS</u> – By living in survival mode, with no sense of the future, gang youth do not care if they engage in future-wrecking behavior. Needing hope just for tomorrow, they do not care about school because it is too future-oriented. A job and bills to pay orients youth to the future and gives hope.

2. <u>HELPLESSNESS</u> - Though in a painful life and lifestyle, gang youth see no possibility of change. A job is a brand new possibility that builds self-esteem and offers a sense of control over your life.

3. <u>INSIGNIFICANCE</u> - Their significant others make them feel insignificant. Father-absent/mother-absent homes produce pain and rage. Graffiti is an attempt by the unrecognized to gain recognition. New significant others must place value on these youth, recognizing the dignity that is already theirs.

4. <u>POVERTY</u> - Where this exists, gangs hold a financial monopoly over youth. Many join a gang for spending money.

A job breaks this stranglehold and is respected by other gang members.

5. <u>FIRST GENERATION IMMIGRANTS</u> - The cultural gap between old country parents and new country youth is vast and often unbridgeable. Many of these youth join gangs for understanding. New responsible adults must provide understanding.

6. <u>FRACTURED FAMILIES</u> - For the love and respect that youth deserve yet don't receive, the gang becomes a perverse substitute family, demanding evil for acceptance. With hearts already filled with pain and rage over their own rejection, unloved youth are only too ready to engage in violent and criminal behavior. New significant others must love and accept these youth as they are, and offer them the opportunity to become part of a new family, God's family.

7. <u>ANGER AT SOCIETY</u> - All of the above wounds create a deep anger misdirected at society. It is too painful to believe that one was unloved and given no rightful place in the world. Caring adults must provide the love that was never there, as well as a job, so that a youth finds a rightful place to harness his energies for the benefit of his own life.

8. <u>TOO MUCH IDLE TIME; TOO FEW RESPONSIBLE ADULTS</u> - With nothing constructive to do, these youth will do nothing constructive. With too few responsible adult role models in their lives, these youth will not become responsible. New significant others and a job put youth in touch with responsible adult role models.

If we do what we have always done, we will only get what we already have.

It's anything but easy being a graffiti vandal, or tagger, living among the bottom dwellers of street life. Hated by gang members for being weak and even by other street artists, they are among the most abandoned, rejected and wounded of youth. Gang members at least have each other, for good or for ill, and will not rat on each other. Graffiti artists usually have nobody – no family and no real friends – and will even lie to get each other in trouble. Although a few may hang together, every graffiti vandal is in competition with every other one. Most gang members are only in competition with rival gangs. A few may use graffiti to advertise their gang affiliation or assert dominance over turf, but gang members have each other and usually live at home with their families. By contrast, many taggers are homeless, having grown up in a ragtag assortment of group and foster homes, never having learned the social skills to get along. Feeling totally unrecognized and of no worth, they paint their tagging nicknames wherever they can, to gain "fame." Hope Now has had much better success working with robbers and murderers than with graffiti vandals.

Gang youth know that crimes and violence are wrong, but they see no other way to survive in their neighborhood, and "everybody needs to survive." The money they earn by selling drugs or stealing is called "dirty money." It makes them feel dirty to earn it. Damon eloquently described his gangbanging days as "making a bad impression on myself!" A real chance to earn "clean money" had never come his way, until Hope Now offered him a job in 1993. Nine years later he still continues to support his family with clean money.

Even success can be bittersweet. When abandoned Jacob passed his driving test, he said, "I wish my Mom could see me." He doesn't know where she is and hasn't for years. Jeffrey's father married again, but his new wife didn't want a teenager around, so Jeffrey slept in the park. Did his father demonstrate caring for his child when he selected his new playmate? Because his mother doesn't care, Jorge has no place to stay. His father has another family now and can't be bothered with his previous litter! Hopeless men sire hopeless boys.

The greatest need in the inner city is for responsible male role models. If there had been responsible male role models of husbands and fathers in the lives of gang young men, most of them would not be in a gang today. In the summer of 1993 our staff went to a park to play basketball with the neighborhood kids. A man pulled up on a motorcycle and one youth said to the other, "Your grandfather's here." The motorcyclist yelled to his grandson to give him an ounce package of cocaine. When his grandson said that all he had that day was marijuana, grandpa demanded, "Be sure to get me some tomorrow!" as he roared off. This is why Hope Now targets transforming the lives of gang young men. If we can turn these youth, many of whom already have children, into responsible husbands and fathers, they will bless both the boys and girls of tomorrow's cities. Young men, furthermore, appear to be the most damaged by the breakdown of their childhood family.

When I attended our son Vue's graduation from Hoover High School, what gave me pause was to notice that only one-fourth of the valedictorians were young men and only one-fourth of the California Federation Scholarship honorees were young men. Since boys and girls appeared to be of approximately equal numbers among the graduates and usually possess similar academic ability, does this indicate that the breakdown of the family is twice as damaging to boys as it is to girls? Poor children of divorced parents most often live with their mothers, which means that girls still have their moms as one role model of a woman. When boys lose daily contact with their fathers, the role model of manhood becomes distant and confused. I have yet to find a poor family that has the means or the organization to execute 50/50 child custody, whatever benefits that may provide. "Custody" among the poor almost always means imprisonment.

Hope Now often receives requests to provide speakers for schools. One teacher asked the students to respond to our challenge to dream about their future, and Gabriel wrote:

I have a pretty good dream! My dream is to
see 20 years of age and to have a good family.
I have a dream that one day I will live peaceful
without fear or thinking that my kids are hurt
or dead. I don't want to have to think that
they are in gangs or on drugs.

I have a dream that one day my father will
get out of prison and be able to see me raise
my children like he could not do for me. I
want to show him that his own son is a really
good father. I have a dream that my children
will know that their father will be somebody
throughout their lives.

Gabriel will need a lot of caring if he is to realize his dream.
He will need a man to care for him before he will know how to
care for his children. We leave our business cards when we
speak, and we pray that youth will call us. It is a long process
to undo a lifetime of neglect and bad choices, but it begins
with a gang youth taking the initiative to contact us, to make
that first investment in change.

With 750 gang youth, ages 16 to 24, placed in jobs with
225 businesses by the end of 2001, new youth are most often
referred by their friends who have gotten jobs. Our staff also
recruits in the streets, parks, malls, and playgrounds. Courthouse Park is a natural place to find youth in trouble. If it's
cold, a couple of counselors will ride the bus and visit with
other youth trying to stay warm. Sometimes we start a conversation on the streets with a request for directions, because
everybody likes to be helpful to a stranger. Then we ask them
what they are doing, if they have a job. If they would like a
job, we tell them that our program helps young men like them,
and hand them a business card. By asking them to call us if
they are interested, they begin the self-selection process of
those who are serious about wanting work. For every ten cards
handed out, we typically get two phone calls, and one of those

two might show up for his first appointment. Alex was one of four young men given cards outside the continuation school where he was going nowhere. When the counselor left, the others threw the cards away, but Alex kept his and made that call. Today he is a very successful bilingual representative for Blue Cross.

If a mother or girlfriend calls seeking help for a young man, we inform her about the program but tell her that the youth himself must call us, must make that first investment in change. Even if he makes the first appointment with his counselor, we don't do an intake, which registers a youth in Hope Now, until he makes the second appointment. By then his counselor knows that he is serious and has a flicker of hope for change. Hope Now also receives referrals from parole and probation officers. Some of our greatest successes have been with California Youth Authority parolees who have spent from three to eight years incarcerated for anything from assault and robbery to manslaughter and murder. Most of our youth are on California Youth Authority parole, California Department of Corrections parole or Fresno County probation. If they have community service to do, we make sure that is taken care of before we place them in a job. By the time we do an intake, he has already begun to climb the first of two simple steps into the American mainstream.

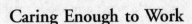

# CHAPTER 5

# Caring Enough to Work

*Two Steps and You're Up: A caring relationship plus a job lift a gang member from the streets into the American mainstream.*

Motto of Hope Now For Youth

One of the most eloquent descriptions of the power of caring comes from the story of a Swedish diplomat, Raoul Wallenberg, who during World War II saved almost 100,000 Hungarian Jews from the Nazis. His method was to show up at deportation centers speaking commanding German and waving official-looking passes, both of which he knew intimidated the Nazi officers. These passes made any Jew holding one into a Swedish citizen under the protection of neutrality. A survivor comments on Wallenberg showing up at a train station:

> *...he gave us hope. He gave us back our dignity, our humanity. Can you fathom the impact of what his being there meant for us? Someone cared, someone who thought we were human beings worth saving. Someone who had no obligation to us fought for us! He saved our lives just by caring for us. We began to care for ourselves.*

Gang members are on a march to prison or death unless someone cares for them.

Adam was born from the rape of a 15-year-old girl by a passing soldier. Because he looked like his father, he became the focus of his mother's anger. Little wonder that Adam didn't get much caring or mothering; this abused and abandoned woman was just trying to survive her own trauma. So Adam didn't care either. He didn't care if he slept in parks or in abandoned buildings for a year while he dealt drugs, just so he could eat. Sometimes he slept half-awake with thousands of dollars and a gun. He didn't care about anything he bought with "dirty" money, leaving clothing, videos and CD's at "friends." A lot of the money went for parties to help him forget the pain of not being cared for. At the end of the year, he owned merely the clothing on his back. For a while, Anthony took Adam in. Anthony's parents would regularly rent a new car and drive to Las Vegas for a weekend of gambling, leaving the boys home with an empty refrigerator. But soon Adam got in an argument with Anthony's dad, so it was back to sleeping in the park. He didn't care.

How do you get someone to begin to care? Remarkably, on a spiritual gifts inventory, all of our staff scored high on the gifts of faith and mercy. Faith enables us to envision and care much about who a young man will become, while mercy allows us to overlook and care little about what he has done. Cared-for children learn to care for themselves. If the significant people in his life treat him as worthwhile, he will see himself as a person of worth. We aim to be those significant adults for each gang youth. When a boy sees himself as a person of worth, he will treat himself and his property with care. Garbage belongs in a landfill; no one puts diamonds there. Trash is found in the streets; diamonds are kept in nice homes with nice people. But a diamond that thinks he's trash, like Adam, will end up in the streets.

It's been well said that I am not becoming what I think I am. I am not becoming what you think I am. But if you are a significant person in my life, *I am becoming what I think you think I am.* Peter was volatile and his name meant pebble, easily moved. But Jesus told him that his name was Boulder, a rock of unswerving faith, and that is what he became. We do not call gang members by their street names, such as Uzi or Cockroach. Using their given names, we offer them a new image. The key to Hope Now's success is to look at gang youth with the eyes of Christ, to care little about the past and much about the future. "I don't care about what you have done. I care very much about what you will do and can do," is what we strive to convey to gang youth. There are five rules for being in Hope Now which help a youth begin to care about himself:

- No lying
- No wearing of colors that announce gang affiliation
- No drugs
- No new crimes
- No new visible tattoos.

As gang members struggle to follow these rules, they are beginning to take care of themselves. Where they see trash, we see diamonds, uncut, unpolished, unset.

Most of the readers of this book have probably been cared for by many significant others: mom, dad, grandparents, aunts and uncles, teachers, coaches, youth directors and pastors. Maybe not all cared, but enough did to make you care about your own future. If the future you were given was sufficiently bright, you more than likely didn't engage in future-wrecking behavior. When we first meet gang members, they believe they have only two futures: prison or death. They believe this not only because they are running dangerous streets and committing violent crimes, but also because their "family" told them that that was their future. They are fulfilling the prophecies made about them, the futures given to them, no matter how horrible.

Maslow developed a hierarchy of needs, with physiological needs such as survival and safety at the bottom and self-actualization at the top. His theory was that you had to fulfill the bottom stages before you could reach the upper stages. Vue, our third son, became a Christian while his opium-smoking mother and brother were starving him. They sold his food stamps and Medi-Cal chits to support their habits. When I asked him if he could think about God when he was hungry, he replied, "When I was hungry, all I could think about was food." Vue wasn't a gang member, but he definitely was at-risk, existing at the level of survival. Several times he returned from school to find a totally empty apartment, with no idea where his family had moved.

Most gang members are living at the level of survival. Once I asked a 16-year-old what he wanted to do when he became an adult. He replied, "I've never really thought about that. I'm just trying to get through today." When your mother is prone to kick you out if her latest boyfriend doesn't like you, you're thinking about where you can spend the night. Since the refrigerator is usually empty, a growing young man goes hungry most of the time and thinks a lot about food. With violence normal in their neighborhoods, many think a lot about not getting killed today. As you can imagine, being in a gang does not lift one's self-esteem. Hector came to us with a neck-lace tattoo exalting his Bulldog gang. It read, "All Dogs Go To Heaven." Our task was to convince him that he's *not* a dog, even though barking is used by this gang to intimidate oth-ers. Later we may have opportunity to persuade him that Jesus is the way to heaven.

Hope Now has found that there is an even more basic need than survival, if a person is ever going to believe he can rise above survival. We call it "significance;" they call it "re-spect." That's why we spend so much individual time with a gang member, caring so they will care. The only antidote to a deficiency of caring, to "I don't care," is caring. Khamsa re-ceived word that his 15-year-old cousin had killed Khamsa's younger brother. Executive Associate John Raymond and Se-nior Vocational Placement Counselor Pe Maokosy stayed in contact with Khamsa to comfort him, and to encourage him not to take revenge but to continue with his successful job. "If it weren't for you guys, I would have killed my cousin," Khamsa said. Then three lives would have been destroyed. To be acces-sible to these youth, our business cards contain not only the business telephone numbers, but also our home phones and pagers. The problems these youth have will not be confined

to conventional business hours: Monday to Friday, 9:00 a.m.
to 5:00 p.m. Like good family, we strive to be available 24/7,
while still making time for our own families. We are often
"there" for them when their families aren't.

Many hours are spent in mentoring and (re)parenting.
The parentheses indicate that many of these youth have not
been adequately parented in the first place. As one youth said,
"You've been like family to us, more than our own family."
Making sure they have a birth certificate, teaching them how
to drive and get a license, accompanying them to court, taking them to emergency medical or dental care, aren't these the
things a parent should do? Sometimes a counselor's caring can
even place him in danger.

A staff member drove to a youth's home after dark, which
is a violation of our Safety Policy, in order to help this young
man resist the temptation of a dealer to sell drugs. When he
arrived, the dealer, the youth, and a kilo of cocaine were there.
Imagine what might have happened if the police had broken
in at that moment! The dealer enjoyed taunting the counselor, "What can you offer me in exchange for my high paying
job? I can buy you!" Even though the counselor didn't know
how to respond, the youth decided not to sell drugs for the
dealer. After reprimanding the counselor for violating our safety
rules, I came up with some possible replies.

### Response to a Challenge
### From a Drug Dealer Making Big Bucks

"What can you offer me in exchange for my high paying
job? I can buy you!"

- I can offer you a better future than prison or death.
- I can offer you dignity and self-respect through legitimate work.
- I can offer you business associates who won't try to kill
  you.
- I can offer you "clean money" that will make your
  grandma smile.

- I can offer you friends who don't expect more back than they give, who won't lie to you and deceive you, and who won't abandon you when you can't pay them back.
- I can offer you a big brother who will be there for you in a crisis.
- I can offer you a good night's sleep and peace of mind.
- I can offer you a real possibility that your little brother won't grow up to be a drug dealer.

Furthermore,

- You can't buy my prayers and concern for you.
- You can't buy my belief that you can change.
- You can't buy the happiness I have in helping my community.
- You can't buy the joy I find in pleasing God.
- You can't buy the certainty of heaven I know in Jesus Christ my Lord.

"He is no fool who gives up what he cannot keep to gain what he cannot lose."

Many gang youth know how to drive but haven't been able to get a driver's license. Since grand theft auto is most often their first major crime, they learn to drive early. The first barrier to being licensed is passing the written test, which for dropouts who can't read well is a formidable undertaking. The counselor's job is to coach him, review old tests, give him a driver's license manual, encourage him to study, and take him for the test. The second barrier to obtaining a driver's license has been formerly insurmountable: finding a fully functional insured vehicle in which to take the road test. The license examiner will ask for proof of car insurance and will check that everything is working. Nobody these youth know has insurance, until now. The counselor allows the youth, after some practice, to take the driving test in the counselor's insured car. Julio failed the driving test for being too cautious. This delightful youth with the engaging smile has a father who tried to kill him twice and a mother who doesn't want him. Is it any wonder he lacks self-confidence? Based on his counselor's confidence in him, however, Julio passed the road test on the second try. Having run away from group homes since he was 14 and ending up in the California Youth Authority, Pablo exulted when he got his license, "This is the first time in my life that I've made any progress!" Youth have cars impounded because they are driving them unlicensed. Obtaining driver's licenses at this point in their lives, however, has one major advantage when it comes to job placement: our employers get youth with clean driving records!

For youth who have worked successfully and still face old warrants or court dates related to earlier crimes or a bad driving record, we are the parent or big brother who accompanies them to court. This often means the difference between going backwards into jail and continuing to go forward with a job. The Lord Jesus goes before us. Executive Associate John Raymond or Training Director Bob Pankratz most often represents us. If I go to court, I wear my reverse clergy collar so that everyone knows that Jesus' representative is in Caesar's lair! We meet some helpful and some hostile deputy district attorneys and public defenders. When John Raymond requested that the public defender ask the judge if John could speak on behalf of Oscar, he replied, "If the sun doesn't rise tomorrow, this judge will want to hear from you!" Since the public defender wouldn't request it, John prayed and stood with Oscar until the judge asked, "Is that your father?" Told that John was from Hope Now, the judge said, "I want to hear from you." Oscar was allowed to continue with his job because, even if the sun doesn't rise, the Son has risen! Because of Jesus' love, caring can arise from where we least expect it.

Each week new Hope Now youth attend Training Time where they learn to relate through conversation and games with our entire staff and with the variety of people they will find in the workplace. As a Black plays chess with a Hispanic, and a Hmong from Laos plays foosball with a white kid from Oklahoma, they discover what their parents never taught them

and their segregated neighborhoods never let them experience
— that we are all human beings with the same needs. And
sometimes there's humor, if a bit macabre. One afternoon
Khoun saw Bong and said, "That's the brother of the guy who
shot me." His counselor asked if he still had hard feelings.
"Oh, no," Khoun replied, "he was aiming for my homie, Joy!"
We're grateful that God had other plans. Joy was named Youth
of the Year at our 2002 annual banquet and helped his brothers find Christ.

Bible studies are also offered each week. Youth are required
to attend two half-hour studies as part of their training. As
Executive Associate John Raymond teaches through the gospels, they learn why we do this ministry and a bit about who
Jesus is. A number of youth continue to attend the Thursday
afternoon studies until they receive a job. Occasionally, a young
man appears to indicate a genuine spiritual interest. Brandon
had held a couple of jobs through Hope Now when he came
back to Bible study the week after 9/11, all shook up. Doing
our best to reassure him, we were happy to give him the Bible
he requested. In January of 2002 he panicked about making a
probation appointment and quit his job without giving notice. In April, Brandon showed up again at Bible study and
said he was sorry to have messed up. Because of the Bible
studies, he said, he had married the mother of his children.
He went on to say, " I'm not here for you guys to get me a job.
I'm here because I need God in my life." Following Bible study,
John was delighted to lead Brandon to the Lord. The basic
aim of these studies is to let the youth know that God cares
about them far more than we do, and that he forgives the
worst things they have done.

Many people who have never met gang members think
that they are all crazy to do the things they do. But gang
members are only trying to meet three normal human needs.
First, there is the need to be cared for, to be part of a family, to
be loved. When asked about his father, Brian said, "I never
met my father. My mother's my father." His brothers were
"all in the dope life." He found in the gang what he never got

at home, and he called it "love." Second, there is the need to succeed at something and be praised. They feel like failures in their broken home, failures in school and failures at getting and holding a job. But they can succeed at crime – they often commit 100 of them before they are caught. And their homies praise them for breaking into a car so fast or burglarizing a store. When he would rob someone, Brian's homies would say, "Good job, Bri. Let's go get budded out." Finally, there is the need for economic reward for effort, because everyone needs money to live and, for a young man, to party. Brian was encouraged to spend some of the money he got by robbery on a pot party with his friends. When they gangbang, they call it, "putting in work." Selling drugs and stealing for the gang meets all these normal needs that should have been met at home.

Carlos had seen his father four times in his 16 years. When he got out of juvenile hall the last time, his mother was too busy trying to please her latest boyfriend to make any place for Carlos to live. His 14-year-old sister just had a baby. Who cares about Carlos? If you saw the tattoos on his legs and the back of his head, it looks like only Satan does. Having finished our training, Carlos finally let his hair grow over the large devil tattooed on his head. Against all odds, Carlos has worked successfully now for two years, has given his heart to the Lord, has gotten involved with a church and is attending college.

A significant number of the Southeast Asian parents in our community carry the scars of the Vietnam War. Having fought for the United States, Choy's father still carries an AK-47 bullet in his brain because removal may render him permanently blind in one eye. His mother has a bullet-shattered knee that incapacitates her. With neither of Choy's parents able to work, it's almost impossible to get on the American economic escalator. That's but one tragic result of the physical scars. And then there are the traumatizing emotional wounds these families carry, devastating losses that inflict pain upon their children. To understand we need only consider the stress disorders still endured by many of our own Vietnam veterans.

Where at all possible, good parents strive to give their

children a good future. Though neither of my parents went to college, I was encouraged and supported to go to college and graduate school. Hope Now aims to give these young men a better future than their parents were able to give them, a future better than prison or death. That broadening future may include success at school and a scholarship for college. But right now, when the need is food on the table and a roof overhead, that better future begins with a better way to earn money – it's called a job.

**CHAPTER 6**

# The Power of a Job

**What a Job Provides**

1) *The only alternative to the streets for getting money*
2) *Personal dignity through earning "clean" money*
3) *Positive role models*
4) *Constructive use of idle time*
5) *A safe environment*
6) *Positive recognition*
7) *Hope for a better future*
8) *Entrance into the American mainstream*

Hope Now Employer Brochure

In May of 1992, following the Los Angeles riots, I saw a television news report about gang members who said that one of the causes of the rebellion was a lack of jobs. Focusing on gang members who had been bussed to northern California to fight forest fires, a reporter asked a 19-year-old African-American how much he was making and how he liked his job. "I'm making $600 a week," he replied. "I could make much more in the gang, but at least when I take this money home I don't have to worry about the cops breaking down my door. And you see this guy over here," he continued, pointing to a Mexican-American, "if we would have met in South Central, we would have tried to kill each other, but here we've become buddies."

As I reflected on that interview, I thought to myself, *"There's the power of a job!"* Not only did a job give that 19-year-old the dignity of earning "clean money," perhaps for the first time, but working with others also broke through his walls of

*51*

racial prejudice, again perhaps for the first time. I was beginning to see that holding a real job for the first time could
indeed be life changing.

The most powerful crime prevention program is still a
job. Parole officials say self-reported figures show unemployment for people entering prison is about 65%, and for ex-
offenders on parole, it is 90% or more. Despite whatever laws
may exist to the contrary, a criminal record is almost always a
bar to employment. Gang youth know that a job is the way
you should earn money, but they don't know how to become
employed. One youth told me that his gang had an annual
"Job Day," where the members would go into fast food businesses and put in applications. When no one got called back,
that justified another year of stealing and selling drugs to survive. Of course, no employer in his right mind would ever
hire these guys. Most are school dropouts, many have tattoos,
their applications are often half completed, and just about all
look like they would kill you. Most have never worked anywhere in the legal economy more than two months. A job
enables an at-risk youth to begin to gain control of his out-of-
control life.

"Years of research show that gainful employment is one of
the best predictors of successful substance abuse treatment,"
stated Substance Abuse and Mental Health Services Administration Acting Administrator Joseph Autry. We find that many
gang youth have used drugs but very few of them prove to be
addicts once they are employed. Larry Freeman, ethics and
professional standards manager for the American Counseling
Association, agrees that vocational training must be within a
comprehensive treatment program than includes a strong support system emphasizing encouragement:

> When one has structure in his life, anxiety
> decreases. It's gratifying to know that one is being
> a productive member in society. But when these
> things, such as a steady job, are not in place, one
> has a lot of opportunities to interact with peers
> who are not in that productive lifestyle.

Training, structure, encouragement, a steady job and a strong support system are the keys to Hope Now's success. At a Bible study, I expressed the view that our staff believes that each man was not there by random choice but by divine appointment, and that we believed that each man could succeed at holding a job. Joseph responded, "I'm glad you believe in us — no one else does."

When Mayor John Street of Philadelphia was asked if an economic boom would largely solve the city's problems, he curtly replied, "It has boomed, and it hasn't solved the problems." He went on to say that much urban poverty is resistant to economic growth because it is rooted not in material deficits but in intangible deficits of the habits, mores, values and dispositions necessary for thriving in an urban society. When gang youth first come to Hope Now, they walk lazy, dress baggy, speak slang, look threatening, sport wild hair and have a bad attitude. They are a perfect fit for the streets and a total misfit for the world of business. Our challenge is to change them into young men who will fill out an application completely and look you in the eye when shaking hands. We know we've succeeded when they pleasantly answer questions like, "Tell me about yourself," speaking in English an employer can understand. Along the path to that job, however, we always offer youth hope so that they will trust us long enough to gain a trusting attitude: a belief in their own ability to hold a job and in our ability to help them find one.

Attitude is the most important ingredient to success over which a gang youth has control. Rev. Charles Swindoll writes in *Strengthening Your Grip:*

> Words can never adequately convey the incredible impact of our attitude toward life. The longer I live the more convinced I become that life is 10 percent what happens to us and 90 percent how we respond to it.
>
> I believe the single most significant decision I can make on a day-to-day basis is my choice of

*attitude. It is more important than my past, my
education, my bankroll, my successes or failures,
fame or pain, what other people think of me or
say about me, my circumstances, or my position.
Attitude keeps me going or cripples my progress.
It alone fuels my fire or assaults my hope. When
my attitudes are right, there's no barrier too high,
no valley too deep, no dream too extreme, no
challenge too great for me.*

The suspicious attitude of many gang members arises from
the untrustworthiness of the important people in their lives.
If we can inspire them to hope long enough and if we prove
trustworthy, they will begin to trust us.

Part of a trusting attitude is the belief that another will
help you. "On the streets, nobody can trust anyone. You can't
believe what anybody says. If someone does something for
you, they expect more back" is what gang members tell us all
the time. So how does Hope Now get them to trust us, to
believe that the only thing we expect back is to see them succeed at a job? Initially there is nothing more important than
arranging an odd job, where a youth has a chance to earn
clean money, perhaps for the first time in his life. If we are
unable to find an odd job for a youth within a week of meeting him, there is a good possibility that we will lose the opportunity to work with that young man. But if he can earn
just $15 of "clean money," hope is inspired and trust begins.

Hope is lifted when a youth realizes that Hope Now is
not "just another government program" that only offers job
training, but rather one where he actually will be placed in a
legitimate job. "Dirty money" from selling drugs or stolen
goods is "easy come, easy go." King Solomon said it well:
*"Wealth from get-rich-quick schemes quickly disappears; wealth
from hard work grows"* (Proverbs 13:11). Some youth earn thousands of dollars but blow it on drug and alcohol parties and at
the end have nothing to show for it. But when Choy earned
his first $20 of "clean money" from an odd job, he made a
payment on the speakers in his car. More importantly, his

belief in his ability to earn money from a job grew.

An odd job is any temporary work of two hours or more that a homeowner or business can offer. As long as the employer has the tools, Hope Now youth provide the labor for yard work, moving furniture, washing windows, or stacking wood while also assisting businesses with inventory or workplace setup. The Vocational Placement Counselor often works alongside the youth to continue to build that male mentoring relationship so vital to job success. Since only the youth is paid, this also gives an extra bonus to the odd job employer. In one of the more interesting odd jobs, a youth spent three weeks assisting in the assembling of an airplane. In another, a woman employed tough-looking Enrique to help her pack for the movers. After two hours of diligent work, Enrique was about to leave when the movers arrived. One look at them and the homeowner asked Enrique to stay – said she'd feel better if he stuck around. Enrique's trust in himself to be good and to do good work were both strengthened that day by this homeowner's trust in him.

In thousands of odd jobs over the last nine years, this supervisor's response has been typical:

> *I want to tell you how impressed I was with the men from Hope Now For Youth. Reuben, Mark, Juan, and Randy helped me with a project over two days. They all worked very hard. They kept busy at all times and I did not have to tell them what to do in order to keep them busy. They sought out work without being told.*

Another ecstatic homeowner left this message before she moved out of town:

> *You sent us three of the best guys I've ever had. They were better than any professional movers we've ever had. They showed up on time or were early, were careful and thorough. I couldn't have asked for anybody better. Thank you for sending us three really neat guys.*

Odd jobs give gang youth the dignity of earning "clean" money, and that's pretty addicting.

Gang youth often tell us, "You trusted me even when I didn't trust myself." Pe Maokosy, now a Senior Vocational Placement Counselor on our staff, tells about his first job – guarding cars in a church parking lot. Pe protested, "Don't you remember? I used to steal cars!" Assured that he was trusted to do the job, he accepted the position and began to see himself in a new light. That first long night, Pe says, he walked around all those fancy cars, looking inside at the steering columns and the stereos, casing them just like he used to. And he thought to himself, "Are they crazy? My own relatives don't want me around their children because I'm a bad influence, yet here these strangers believe that I will guard the cars I used to steal." That trust, Pe says, changed the direction of his life. Because he was trusted, Pe began to trust himself to do the right thing.

When Senior Vocational Placement Counselor Robert Rubio and I visited Edgar on his front porch, he expressed gratefulness for his part-time night janitorial position at the Sanger Bank of America. Here was an opportunity to change from his gang lifestyle and provide for his daughter. "My homies can't believe it. They can't believe that I have the keys to the Bank of America!" he chuckled. Trustworthiness is built by being trusted, and we find that these men are eager to prove themselves worthy of our trust.

Getting ready for a job also involves having the proper identification and training. The chaos of their unparented homes often does not allow youth to keep track of birth certificates or Social Security cards. Some report that their wallets were stolen and they lost their California ID or other photo identification. So our staff helps them reestablish the necessary identification to obtain a job. This may involve writing to a distant state or standing with them in line at 5:00 a.m. waiting for the Immigration and Naturalization Service Office to open.

Each young man is put through a series of one-on-one

and group classes to build that all-important positive caring relationship as well as to impart information and Judeo-Christian values. Job Success teaches him how to keep a job, including dealing with fellow employees and difficult employers. Job Search teaches him how to fill out an application and conduct himself in an interview. To try to minimize family disruptions of job performance, Job Support supplies tools to build positive relationships at home. Wisely budgeting and spending the money he has earned is the subject of Job Finance.

Drug and Alcohol Addiction Awareness enables the youth to do a self-evaluation of any addictive tendencies, to identify what is truly abnormal in contrast to his environment in which addiction may be the norm. To enable each youth to understand the source of his anger and allow God to heal him is the subject of the sixth class, Anger Recognition and Release. About ten percent of our youth find a job on their own during or after completing Hope Now training. Following completion of his training, Anthony was beaming from ear to ear when he said, "I got my own job at Mervyn's and I am the first employee to get 10 written compliments from customers!"

What can you give to youth who are so angry and hopeless that they believe they have nothing to lose? Desperation can even be an ally, as Alberto expressed it, "All my friends are dead, in jail or getting a job from Hope Now for Youth. I want a job." Hope Now finds that a helping friendship and a job are two things that gang youth do *not* want to lose. Joe and Derek were working successfully through Hope Now when they entered an aisle of the local discount store and came face to face with Edgar, also with Hope Now. Given their rival gang histories of shootings and stabbings, the next announcement might have been, "Attention, K-Mart shoppers! There's a bloodbath on Aisle 9!" But they decided not to fight each other any more because all were employed through Hope Now and they didn't want to risk losing their jobs.

When we give these youth some things worth *not* losing, they begin to care about themselves and their future. And once they begin to care about their future, gang members gradually understand that Hope Now is really offering them a way out of their miserable circumstances. It can be an adrenaline rush to gangbang, staying ahead of the police, but most of the time the gang lifestyle fills you only with dread and despair. Watching your back, always hypervigilant for a rival's revenge, not trusting anyone, while constantly running from police produce unrelenting stress that is only temporarily relieved by partying. Getting high or drunk only adds to the problems.

The fundamental problem every gangbanger sooner or later is trying to solve is, "How do I get enough money to survive?" Everyone needs money to live. What is painfully obvious to poor kids is often not an issue for those of us who have always had money. When speaking in churches, I often stress the importance of a job by asking, "How many of you would be worshipping God here this morning if you didn't have a job or the fruits of a job like Social Security or investments?" When no hands go up, several points can be clarified. First, everyone needs money to live. Second, until the economic problem is solved, it is difficult to deal with the spiritual need. And finally, the needs of gang youth are no different than our own needs. They just want to know how to meet them in legitimate ways. Tou was such a good worker that McDonald's sent him to Florida to train the crew of a new restaurant. When Tou became a shift manager, he introduced Executive Associate John Raymond to his crew with these words, "These people helped me when I was on the floor." Wouldn't we all be on the floor without a job?

But getting legitimate businesses to hire gang youth was more of a challenge than I bargained for. When asked in 1993 how job availability was going, I would reply, "It's like pushing an elephant uphill." Cleaning out dog kennels was one of the better jobs we found, until God brought us a break. In December, my pastor, Dr. Douglas J. Rumford of First Presbyterian Church, invited me to be one of three speakers for a Rotary Club of Fresno Christmas program. Not until I arrived did I realize that I was speaking to almost 400 of the movers and shakers of our community. In my five minutes, I chose to describe Christmas for a poor gang kid, with no presents under the tree, probably no tree at all, and an unending need to hustle money for the next day. Before and during my talk, I was praying that someone's heart would be broken for the violent children who were pushing Fresno to 97 homicides that year. I was not to be disappointed.

The Lord not only brought me an employer, but he brought the "Mercedes Benz" of employers to my table at the conclusion of the meeting. Rex Riley, Chief Operating Officer of Valley Children's Hospital, explained that what we were trying to do with gang youth fit into the mission of the hospital. Following that December conversation, Valley Children's Hospital created four training slots just for Hope Now youth. On March 1, 1994, we took four at-risk and gang youth to work at Valley Children's Hospital, including one young woman from the Calvary Vocational Placement Program. Eight years later, Hok, the first young man we ever placed in a job, is a Plant Utility Engineer who has married the mother of his children and is buying a home. And in 2000, after leaving the hospital in September of 1994 for work in North Carolina, Mang showed up in an expensive suit and yellow-tinted glasses to let us know that he was a successful furniture salesman. Miguel worked for a year at the hospital but, soon after he left, we lost track of him.

The story of how we placed Karina, the female of the foursome, is the most instructive. When told about the job, she was all excited. But when telephoned two days before the interview, she was all tears. Her grandmother did not want Karina to take the job because the family would lose about $200 in monthly welfare payments. It didn't compute in her grandmother's welfare experience that Karina would be making $800 per month, which would more than make up the shortfall. Within three generations, welfare had become the way to survive. One more attempt to set Karina free had to be tried. She was asked to put her younger brother, Oscar on the phone. Oscar was the determined negotiator, wearing down friend and foe alike with unending arguments. So Oscar was offered $20 if he could convince his grandmother to let Karina take the job. Of course, he eagerly accepted the challenge. Oscar earned my hilarious respect as well as the $20 when Karina called and said her grandmother agreed that she could go to work. Even before Karina went on to work for five years at Valley Children's, I knew that that $20 was the best investment ever made.

Some inner city organizations working with at-risk youth strive to develop entrepreneurship and micro enterprises. I have found that more organizations are talking about self-directed businesses than are actually establishing them. Even if entrepreneurships or micro businesses are formed, they are unable to employ a large number of youth. Of course, some inner city youth don't want to work for the "man." No doubt many gang youth have leadership abilities, but we don't assume that business skills can be developed only in self-employment. Learning to work for someone else is a vital step in learning how to have someone work for you. Good businesses are always training for management. And if we don't help youth get over their generic hostilities toward the "man," we will never prepare them for the larger world of business. One final impediment to our pursuing the entrepreneurship model was the need our youth had for medical and dental benefits for themselves and their families. Self-directed enterprises usually are not large enough to provide such benefits.

In July of 1994 the Fresno Business Council, comprised of the CEO's of the 125 largest corporations in the Fresno area, enthusiastically endorsed Hope Now to its member businesses. Bob Carter, the founder and first president of the Council, wrote,

> *Many of us have searched for ways to make a difference in the seemingly intractable problem of crime in our community. Hope Now has developed a program for kids that works. By combining a family-type relationship with a job*

> *opportunity, Hope Now has provided a choice, a*
> *path into the mainstream, for kids without a*
> *future.*

On a hot day in September of 1996, when we had just started Hope Now in Sanger, I accompanied Senior Vocational Placement Counselor Robert Rubio while recruiting on the Norteno (northern California gang) side of town. We found three guys standing in a dirt lot near a convenience store, under the welcome shade of a fig tree. One of them was already drunk from sipping the cheap wine in the brown paper bag he held. Another was too young, still too enthralled with gangbanging, and seemed disinterested. And then there was Isaiah – intelligent, interested, a high school graduate raised up in gang ghetto life. Robert tried working with him, but Isaiah seemed determined to "fail, jail and bail." He lasted one month in the only job we got him. But in 2000 he entered college, found his own job and became the first Hope Now youth to hire another Hope Now youth at an auto body shop. Isaiah now believes he has a future.

Once Valley Children's Hospital, now named Children's Hospital Central California, had hired our youth and had good results, the doors began to open to the business community. Their good name worked wonders for the youth of Hope Now. But we were to discover that finding a job for a gang youth, as difficult as that is, was not nearly as hard as helping that youth keep his job.

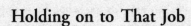 

# CHAPTER 7

# Holding on to That Job

*Don't be fooled by me. Don't be fooled by the face I wear. I wear a mask. I wear a thousand masks — masks that I am afraid to take off; and none of them is me. Pretending is an art that is second nature to me, but don't be fooled. For my sake, don't be fooled. I give the impression that I am secure, that all is sunny and unruffled within me as well as without, that confidence is my name and coolness my game, that the water is calm and I am in command, and that I need no one.*

Anonymous

If a Hope Now youth can hold a job for 30 days or longer, we consider him a success. By this initial measure, over 80% of our trained youth are successful. Even if a young man loses his job after a month, he has learned something he probably never knew before: there is an alternative to the streets for earning money. He also has learned what it was that made him lose his job, such as missing days or being late. Hope Now youth miss too many days or are late too many times for a variety of reasons.

Many of our youth have criminal records that dog them. A record often starts with a GTA, grand theft auto. To our knowledge, only one had a record that included GTC, grand theft cow. Nith and his friends wanted to have a barbeque but had no meat, so one of his homies suggested, "Let's go shoot a cow." Nith told us he didn't want to do it, but he wasn't going to stand against the tide. After helping them bring it back, Nith butchered it and they all had a great time. The next day, they all were arrested. As we were about to place

Nith in a permanent job, he told us there was a warrant out on him because he had failed to make a court appearance. Incidents like these helped us to focus first on clearing up a youth's bad past while still pointing him toward a good future.

A gang youth can lose his job when he is caught in a traffic stop and an old warrant pops up on the officer's computer screen. For that infraction, at least a week in jail and the loss of his job is standard procedure, so now we check with the Fresno County Sheriff's Department for warrants before we place a youth. Many times, the youth doesn't even know he has a warrant, and sometimes the warrant has been issued in error. In either case, however, if a youth is picked up on a warrant, jail time and job loss are usually inescapable. Many warrants are for missing a previous court date. Even for more serious matters, if a youth turns himself in, most times he is not jailed. Hope Now policy is that all warrants must be cleared before a youth is placed in permanent employment. That means we may accompany him to the courthouse to set a hearing date and may even provide him an attorney. We must do whatever is necessary to remove this impediment to future success.

Nith's story contains another significant reason why a youth will lose a job: keeping his old associates who still have the old lifestyle with nothing to lose. If Nith does not find friends among other youth who are at least holding a job, he will get in trouble again. At a party, a person who has no job to lose and no self-respect to ruin will get drunk enough to encourage others to join him in committing a crime. Sometimes homies come by the house and invite the Hope Now youth to go joyriding in a stolen car or do a beer run on a convenience store. If our young man has learned enough, he'll tell them that he has to get up early to go to work, so he can't run the night with them.

When we met Pon, he had a job but didn't having caring relationships, so he had been arrested with the wrong friends in a stolen car. When we went to court with him, the judge granted a conditional plea: if Pon stayed out of trouble for one year the charges would be dismissed. Pon performed community service and also paid the insurance deductible on the stolen auto. When the year ended we went to court with Pon again. The probation officer reported, "He went beyond the call of duty." In dismissing the charges, the judge said, "Good job, young man, and good luck." The problem of wrong associates is greatly magnified, however, when they live in your own home.

A person who continues to go back to the girlfriend who got him in trouble, we call a "moth." If there is one primary reason why a youth cannot hold a job, it is family problems, specifically with a girlfriend or the mother of his children. George's girlfriend continued to flirt with her last boyfriend. Using the only way he knew to cope with frustration, George pushed her so hard she almost fell down an entire flight of stairs. Neighbors called the police and George was locked up, eventually serving 17 months. He had worked at his Hope Now job all of one day. When George got out of prison we warned him not to go back to his girlfriend, put him through retraining, including some anger management, and placed him in another job. After working for two months, he was laid off. We heard he was back with his old girlfriend again, and even got her pregnant. Two months later, he hit her again and went back to prison. George was a moth; we dropped him from our program.

Spousal abuse is not the only family problem that pulls youth from the path to success. Abusive mothers offer another fatal detour. Because not being loved by one's mother is too horrible to contemplate, abused young men tragically conclude that the following aberrations mean they are loved:

- Abandoning him for her drug or gambling habit
- Kicking him out because her latest boyfriend doesn't like him
- Selling his only work transportation, a bike, to finance her drug habit
- Hitting him up for money every payday
- Teaching him how to shoplift and hold his liquor by age 12
- Telling him he'll be dead or in prison by age 18, like his loser father

· Ignoring him while she's partying, so he gets molested in the back bedroom

· "Disciplining" him with a fist, shoe, cable, broom handle, or thrown telephone

· Saying she wishes that he were never born, that she had gotten an abortion.

Ironically, when Mother's Day comes, this rejecting unfit caricature of a mother expects and receives undeserved attention, adulation and gifts from her victim. As incredible as that may seem to us, it is even more inconceivable to the young man to think that he was never loved, never wanted at all.

Too often the patterns of exploitation and subjugation carved into a youth interfere with making a new life through legitimate employment. For example, when this self-absorbed mother gets sick and needs to go to the doctor, our newly placed employee is expected and feels duty-bound to take her. He misses a whole day of work for chauffeur duty that few employers would excuse, even if asked, and then wonders why he was fired. To help a youth build a different future as a dependable employee, we tell him to find someone else in the family who is not employed to take her to the doctor. Continuous mentoring is required to extract these youth from the morass of victimization and neglect that sabotages all their relationships.

A pregnant girlfriend will also have to find her own way to medical care. If he argues with her, she will throw him out of the apartment paid for by her other children's welfare. Again our young man has another excuse for not going to work, and subsequently losing his job. Without the stability and commitment of marriage, chaotic relationships are the norm. They don't get married, they tell us, because there is no economic base from which to build a sustainable relationship. Having a violent argument with his latest girlfriend over his previous one is fairly common. In his childhood home, as well as hers, arguments were usually "settled" by physical violence. That blowup with a girlfriend is enough to keep him from going to work and may even land him in jail, where he stares at the ceiling of his cell trying to sort out his rage.

Koy was only nine years old when left in charge of five younger brothers and a sister, cooking meals, and making sure they got to school and back. Mom and Dad, casino employees with different shifts, were always asleep, there but not there. When they weren't sleeping, they were gambling away the food and clothing money, sometimes for 48 hours at a crack. By the time he was 14, Koy had dropped out of the ninth grade to care for his siblings, but nobody cared for him. Nobody took him fishing, nobody helped him get an education. His parents only used Koy to parent for them.

Koy missed work and lost his job because he was angry at having to parent six other family members. John and I counseled Koy to release his anger at the Cross by giving his heart to Jesus, but he was not ready. The day before Thanksgiving, Koy told John that he had prayed to receive Christ in "English, Cambodian and street language." Isn't it great to serve a multilingual God? On Saturday a friend invited Koy to a roller rink but "a voice in my head told me not to go." That night his friend was shot. When Vocational Placement Counselor Yue Pheng Vang heard about it, he contacted Keo and Thea who, in the past, would have retaliated. Both of them had jobs through Hope Now, so we were delighted when Keo said, "I have too much to lose now," and neither youth retaliated. We want to do everything to make sure a youth does not lose his job.

Hope Now provides alarm clocks for those homes with none, so that excuses for being late are minimized. The greatest work-related failure of our youth, however, is "missing too many days." When you have never experienced the benefits of a regular job, when regular work has never been modeled in your home, there is no urgency to do the things necessary to stay employed. Lacking a responsible family structure, there is no backup when your car breaks down, no one to encourage you to keep on keeping on. Another missed day is the result. Even a 15-minute doctor's appointment becomes a reason for missing an entire day of work. They have never had to be consistently accountable before – why start now? The answer lies in their almost miraculous desire to hold a job.

Toy had worked only one day when it was decided to fire him because he was too slow. The temporary service that placed him was notified, but because they never got around to telling Toy, he just kept coming to work. A week later the foreman told Human Resources what a great job Toy was doing. "Toy? He was supposed to be fired!" the director exclaimed. Toy continued to work, all fired up. Nathan, doing Christmas tree pickup for the City of Fresno, walked five miles at 3:00 am to the city yard. We gave him a donated bicycle. Richard broke the pedal off his donated bicycle in a collision with a car, so he biked the remaining three miles to work using one pedal, still arriving early enough to wake up the night watchman! Marshall, who lost his car transportation, bicycled 11 miles each way to a graveyard shift at Clovis Community Hospital. We see just how badly gang youth want to become miracles, but so much drags them back into the chaos.

The developed lifestyle of gang youth is reactive, not proactive. With the possible exception of scheming revenge or crimes, they respond to situations instead of planning them. On jail visits, I have often told a young man, "Your problem is that you just let life happen *to* you instead of making life happen *for* you." It really is a miracle of God when a gang youth shows up to work on time five days a week, because that is the first and only planned and regular activity in his life since he dropped out or was kicked out of school. This pervasive lack of planning is further demonstrated when a staff member makes a social appointment with them to go fishing, to a dinner or to a show. Even confirming the day before and calling two hours ahead does not guarantee that the young man will be there when it is time to pick him up. He may have forgotten to come home from a previous reaction, or his cousin came by 20 minutes before you did and they went out. Little wonder that our attempt to get adult volunteers to be mentors for these youth went nowhere except to discouragement. I pay my staff to continue to pursue even when they are stood up and disappointed.

So that gang youth do not see themselves as disappointments, we provide new definitions of success and failure that encourage them to hold on to that job. We begin with Dr. Robert Schuller's definition: " Failure is not aiming at a high goal and falling short; failure is aiming at nothing and succeeding." Holding a job is a high goal for a gang youth and, even if he fails to hold the first one, it doesn't mean he's a failure. Committing a crime or getting drunk or high is a failure even if the youth succeeds. This poem describes the values of success and failure we try to inculcate.

### FAILURE IS NEVER FINAL
#### Author Unknown

Failure is never final!
The only time I can't afford to fail
    is the very last time I try.
Failure doesn't mean I'm a failure;
It just means I haven't succeeded.

Failure doesn't mean I have accomplished nothing;
It just means I've learned something.
Failure doesn't mean I've been a fool;
It just means I had faith enough to experiment.

Failure doesn't mean I've been disgraced;
It just means I dared to try.
Failure doesn't mean I don't have what it takes;
It just means I must do things differently next time.

Failure doesn't mean I'm inferior;
It just means I'm not perfect.
Failure doesn't mean I've wasted my time;
It just means I have reason to start over.

Failure doesn't mean I should give up;
It just means I should try harder.
Failure doesn't mean I'll never make it;
It just means I need more patience.

Failure doesn't mean I'm wrong;
It just means I must find a better way.
Failure doesn't mean God has abandoned me;
It just means I must diligently seek His will!

For young men existing at the level of survival, it is vital to convince them that a job can lift them above survival. After receiving a few paychecks, their view of the significance of a job grows. The experience of earning clean money translates into dignity and self-worth found in no other way. Tim had been locked up in juvenile hall for carjacking. There he earned most of his high school credits. When his Hope Now counselor took Tim along to wrestling practice, Tim confided that he needed a job to take his girl to the prom. His dad was nowhere to be found, and he couldn't depend on his crack-addicted mom. Whenever she got some money, she would disappear for a couple of days and come home broke.

During the next few weeks, his counselor placed Tim in odd jobs while continuing to give him positive feedback. Before Tim even finished our training classes, he found his own job. After he turned 18, we placed him at Fresno Community Hospital, he graduated from high school, and today Tim is our first United States Marine. From dignity to self-worth to Semper Fi — Tim was correctly convinced that working, getting his diploma, earning a felony waiver and then entering military service was a way to get above survival in a crack-home. From the juvenile hall worker to the fast food manager, from the homeowners offering odd jobs to the hospital department supervisor, from a helpful attorney to the United States government, it takes everybody doing their part to lift at-risk youth into the mainstream. Working together we aim to make every employer as satisfied as this Human Resources Manager at Mount Vernon Mills:

> Hope Now is a great organization that offers so much, not only to the young men, but also to the business community. They are my first choice for employees, because the youth have a wonderful support group to help them succeed – and to help our business succeed.

The primary support group is the Hope Now staff, but members of the secondary team include everyone with a heart to heal wounded youth.

# CHAPTER 8

# It Takes a Village

*All of the children of the community will take from the time, talents and resources of the community, one way or another. Either they will get these up front in nurture or later in punishment.*

Dr. Deborah Prothrow-Stith
Harvard Medical School

When I announced my resignation from the pastorate of Pilgrim Armenian Congregational Church to start Hope Now For Youth, members of one parish family approached me individually with, amazingly, the same message: "We're sorry to see you go, but are excited about what you will be doing. If there is any way we can help, please let us know." Aram and Barbara Garabedian and I had not always agreed on every decision made by the church, but we consistently stood together on helping young people, and now, gang youth. Their son, Dale, a certified public accountant, was equally committed as was their daughter, Robyn Esraelian, an attorney. Working through Abaci & Garabedian, Certified Public Accountants, and Richardson, Jones and Esraelian, Attorneys at Law, Dale and Robyn have donated all Hope Now corporation accounting, tax services and legal services since 1992, including incorporating and obtaining our federal and state tax exempt status. Robyn has also obtained pro bono services from a score of other attorneys to assist Hope Now youth with everything from child support to dealing with past warrants. In a criminal matter, the difference between having a competent attorney or not is often the difference between receiving a jail sentence or another chance. There is more equitable justice for those who have personal attorneys. As we speak about

Hope Now to various groups, new professionals come forward to assist us.

Marcos had a girlfriend who was an illegal alien, a baby and no money. He couldn't find a job with a future. Before he found Hope Now, he considered selling drugs to survive. Marcos didn't have a great start in life: "I don't know my father. All I know about him is that he was a drinking man and when I was a little boy he wanted to kill me." We placed him at a job in 1995, found an attorney to help his wife get legal status, and today Marcos is a journeyman mechanic rebuilding truck drivelines. Attorney Mike Splivalo had never handled immigration problems, but took up the challenge to learn. We love to offer mind-expanding and heart-enlarging experiences to the village. When a physician gravely informed Mama Miller, a saintly friend of mine, that she had an enlarged heart, she exclaimed, "Oh, doctor, that's wonderful news! Now I can tuck more people into my heart!" An enlarged heart is one of the risk factors for anyone who helps at-risk youth.

To keep urgent health problems from interfering with the ability to work, physicians, dentists, and oral surgeons donate emergency services to Hope Now youth for anything from a severe rash to an aching wisdom tooth. A pre-employment physical examination may uncover the need for glasses, which optometrists donate. Most poor youth have had no dental care for years, and certainly no preventive care. Looking into one man's mouth to try to determine what was hurting, I was stunned and saddened to see one tooth destroyed down to the level of the gum and only a pinnacle where another used to be. How important it is to get these youth into jobs with benefits for themselves and their families, and then to teach them how to use these benefits preventively.

Not usually covered by health insurance, tattoo removal was a cosmetic medical need we tried to meet early on. A youth trying to change his lifestyle sometimes feels hampered by visible gang or prison tattoos on face, neck, arms or hands. The latest rage seems to be the totally tattooed head that, fortunately, can be covered by hair. Tattoos have not been a hindrance to job placement with most light industrial employers, but they do permanently brand an individual as belonging to one gang even if he wants out. In the wrong setting, and if he's got the wrong attitude, tattoos can cause trouble. Making an arrangement with Dr. Jane Kardashian, a local dermatologist, Hope Now initially obtained donations of both her professional services and of the laser rental time to remove tattoos from several youth from March of 1996 through July of 1999. During the last half of that period, we were paying about half the cost. Gary Ohanesian at Gary's All-Med Drugs donated the topical anesthetic and the antibiotic cream required throughout this period, and has since contributed other needed prescriptions.

The major problem with tattoo removal for gang youth is that it is not a one-time procedure. Anywhere from four to six laser treatments are required depending on the type, size or color of the tattoo, and these normally are spaced six weeks apart. Following treatment the skin is blistered and must be covered for a day or more to prevent infection. Sometimes that meant a young man was unable to do his work and would lose pay. What was most difficult, however, was finding the youth for each of the treatments and making sure they got to the physician's office. Rarely would they remember their appointments. Although Roy, Timmy, Kip, and Vang certainly benefited from showing up for most of their treatments, many did not show up enough times to justify our expense. Once Senior Vocational Placement Counselor Robert Rubio completed his tattoo removal treatments, the sporadic participation of Hope Now youth no longer warranted further investment of staff time. When in the summer of 1999 University Medical Center offered a state-sponsored program for gang members to remove tattoos, we happily referred youth there. Unfortunately, the grant was not in the State of California's budget for the following year, leaving a $40,000 laser idle and gang youth branded. The irony is that that money may have gone to build new prison facilities.

After spending 22 years feeling and often being responsible for church facilities worth up to two million dollars, the last thing I wanted to do in Hope Now was to be responsible for more buildings, grounds and vehicles. As I looked at the young men I felt called to help, it was obvious that these were not what they needed. What they needed were relationships of hope and help. We could offer these without facility rent, utility bill or van maintenance. This was a Christian ministry which could and should operate out of Christian churches which have otherwise empty Sunday School facilities during the business week. If churches would adopt Hope Now as one of their ministries to the community, we would have all the physical space we needed. Today seven churches  donate space and utilities, usually including telephone, to enable our counselors to meet with gang youth: First Presbyterian, Fresno; University Presbyterian; Butler Avenue Mennonite Brethren; Crosspoint Southern Baptist; West McKinley Assembly of God; First Presbyterian, Sanger; and Family Worship Center. Older management staff members like myself, without young children to distract, operate from a home office. We've got to take care of our homes and pay our own utilities anyway.

Weekly staff meetings are held around the dining room table in my home, corporate headquarters for Hope Now For Youth. Volunteers help prepare the monthly newsletter for bulk mailing at that same table. Churches donate their fellowship halls for Thanksgiving and Christmas Family Dinners. Church members and Fresno Pacific University open their retreat and beach homes for staff conferences. The University also donates its courtyard, swimming pool and gymnasium for our annual barbeque and three-on-three basketball tournament. Hidden from the street, their campus is a safer place for ex-gang members and their families to gather than a public park.

Once people get the idea that gang members can be changed, it seems everybody wants to help. Drug Testing Resource furnishes drug tests at cost. As already mentioned, homeowners provide hundreds of odd jobs each year. Occasionally we will put requests for odd jobs in church newsletters. Homeowners also supply us with used men's bicycles to transport youth back and forth to work. If these bicycles need to be fixed, Cyclopath bike shop donates repairs. Early on, we only provided bicycles, but soon discovered that they were being stolen, so now we also provide u-bar bike locks, purchased at cost from Cyclopath. B & L Mechanical donated 10 new bicycles one Christmas, and Toys-R-Us contributed bicycle assembly. The bikes are kept in a storage locker donated by Derrel's Mini Storage. The locker also contains furniture donations available to both youth and street staff.

Owner Eric Kozlowski began hiring our youth in his direct-mailing center in 1995. Today, almost all printing is donated by Consolidated Printworks, a division of the Presort Center. Dumont Printing annually donates a four-color brochure used with new employers and for public relations. Web site (www.hopenow.org) hosting and marketing is donated by AltaPacific. We encourage our businesses to become Community Plus Employers by hiring Hope Now youth and donating at least $1000 annually to further the program. Like The Presort Center, some choose to donate goods or services instead. The Radisson Hotel and Conference Center hosts the annual banquet at reduced cost.

Award plaques provided at cost by Omega Trophy are presented to the Community Plus Employers at each banquet. Awards are also presented to youth who have worked one year and five years. For most, who have never graduated from high school, the one-year award is the first framed recognition of achievement they have ever received. Each awardee also receives a Bible donated by the Lockman Foundation. Engraved watches donated by Warner Co. Jewelers are presented to those youth who have worked successfully for five years. Circuit City provides a gift certificate for the Hope Now Youth of the Year chosen by the staff.

Over the years, JC Penney and Sears have provided gift certificates to help youth obtain any specialized clothing or shoes they may need for work. The staff has Hope Now caps and shirts provided by J&J Monograms of Tucson. Great Escape Travel provided a 29-passenger bus for a beach trip. At Thanksgiving, turkeys are donated for youth families by Zacky Farms. The United States Marines collect from the community and supply us Toys for Tots at Christmas and Fresno Plumbing and Heating hands out coupons for free Christmas trees. For conferences or trips away, our supporters offer vans and suburbans.

Childcare is volunteered for the Family Dinners by the junior high and high school students of Pilgrim Way Academy with adult supervision. They have had as many as 53 kids to watch! My wife, Marilyn, enlists me to join her in food preparation, and other volunteers supply serving and cleanup. Staff wives also team with us to teach Marriage and Family Classes, Parenting Classes and Bible studies. Many individuals and organizations have contributed staff training. The Performance Link and Empowerment Strategies have donated staff team building and board development retreats.

My wife, who has been bookkeeper and telephone receptionist out of our home since the beginning, has probably done the greatest amount of volunteering. In opening our home as the headquarters of Hope Now, including for meetings and mailings, Marilyn has shown a significantly enlarged heart toward hurting youth. That largesse was truly tested when in 1993 I brought home "for a couple of days" a 15-year old Hmong boy who had been abandoned by his opium-smoking mother and brother. While he was trying to attend high school, they were starving him by selling his food stamps for their habits. This was the third time I knew of that he had come home to an empty apartment. Currently completing his college education in Information Systems, today Vue Lee is the third son in our home and our hearts. If you don't think receiving an instant teenager into your home is not challenging, you've never tried it.

The love behind all this generosity of spirit toward hurting youth is immeasurable, but the annual dollar value comes to around $150,000. The hope for gang youth that is vibrant in Fresno, I am convinced, lies dormant throughout our nation. It costs Hope Now $5,000 to change the life direction of one gang young man for many years but we are taxed $50,000 to incarcerate and adjudicate that same young man for one year, only to have him turn out worse. You are making an investment in every gang member in your community. The only choice you have is where and when to make your investment. In every city there are caring homeowners, employers, church members, politicians, and peace officers who want to help kids go straight, but don't know what to do. Some have tried and have been burned, yet most still want to help a gang member take that first step in the right direction. That first step will positively affect many others and perhaps many generations.

# CHAPTER 9

# A Real Man for His Family

*I believe and maintain that if culturally focused/politically clear and responsible Black fathers were a majority in the African-American family and community, there would not be a gang, drug or crime problem at the level that exists today. This is not to suggest that gangs, drugs or crime would not exist in our communities, but it is to state that gangs, drugs and crime would not rule or run our communities as they now do in too many instances. Fathers in working families do make a difference; Black women against great odds are fighting a losing battle, and responsible and dependable fathers, grandfathers, uncles and men of our extended family are critically needed.*

Haki R. Madhubuti
*Why L.A. Happened*

Manhood is defined by most cultures as the ability to protect and provide for one's family, but gang members define manhood as gaining "respect" through intimidation, scoring with girls by deceit, and having babies any way they can. Hope Now teaches young men that all it takes to become a father is sperm, but it takes a lifetime to be a dad. Since most of them never had a dad, we have to help them fill in the gaps. It's hard to be a parent if you have not been adequately parented, so Hope Now does a great deal of (re)parenting. Our older staff members model what a good father does, protecting and providing for each youth. When Vocational Placement Counselor Eddie Ochoa started as a youth in our program, he told us, "You're the first ones to teach me right from wrong." That's what a good father does.

If you examine Eddie's life transformation in his own words, you will understand what possibilities a fathering/mentoring relationship and a job can unlock:

> I was brought up in a home that for the first ten years of my life was dysfunctional. Living on the southeast side of town also contributed to my negative upbringing. While I was growing up, there were drugs, alcohol and verbal abuse in my family. This lifestyle caused me to act out at a young age.
>
> When I was ten years old, my criminal record began with breaking a window. By the time I was 13, I was stealing cars, smoking weed and getting into trouble at school. As I turned 16, I began to associate with known gang members, and to sell drugs. Since I had found out that my girlfriend was pregnant, selling drugs was the only way I thought I could make some money fast.
>
> I began selling drugs in my neighborhood with my friends. We started to make some money, but were also taking business from some rival gang members. As a result they declared war on us. All I could remember was that we were hanging out in front of my friend's house and a car pulled up. Three older guys came out. One of them hit me and pulled out what looked like a 9mm weapon. When I saw the weapon, I ran into my friend's house.
>
> My friends were talking about retaliating. As I began to realize the severity of the situation, I thought about my girlfriend and my baby. I didn't want my baby to grow up without a father. I knew the result of retaliating would be my death or imprisonment, so I got out of

the situation by relocating to my girlfriend's house on the north side of town.

Moving to my girlfriend's house helped for a little while until things cooled down, but I still didn't learn my lesson. I began selling drugs again to get money to survive. I didn't see a way out, because this lifestyle was all I knew. I had dropped out of school, had a baby and didn't have any sense of direction in my life. I wanted to change but didn't know how.

One day I was watching TV and saw one of the friends I used to run with on the news. He was talking about Hope Now For Youth and about how much it changed his life. The next day I called and spoke to Roger Minassian. Roger assigned me to a counselor named Alex Arellano. Alex and I worked together in a few odd jobs, but more importantly, we built a relationship.

Alex gave me positive feedback and said there was another way of life. As a result I began to feel good about myself and gained the confidence to go out and get my own job at a fast food restaurant. I worked there for about six months.

In 1995, Hope Now got me a job at Holiday Inn Centre Plaza, where I stayed for about a year. During that time I went back to school for my GED. After seeing the changes that only God could have brought to my life, I gave my heart to follow Jesus. When Alex and Roger asked if I would like to work for Hope Now, I was thrilled to have the opportunity to give back to the community and to help other young gang members look at life from a different perspective.

On June 10, 1996, I became a Vocational
Placement Counselor for Hope Now. Since
then I've gotten married to the mother of my
children, obtained my GED, bought a home,
and received my A.A. degree from Fresno City
College. Currently I am enrolled in the Management and Organizational Development
program at Fresno Pacific University and hope
to receive my B.A. in 2003. Hope Now has
been a blessing in my life. I truly believe that
without this organization I would be in prison
or dead.

Eddie is too modest to tell you that when he was doing
laundry at the Holiday Inn Centre Plaza, I received rave re-
views on his work. His supervisor said, "If you get me ten
more like Eddie, I'll fire the other 40!" As a Hope Now counselor, Eddie has helped almost 175 gang members "look at
life from a different perspective." We helped his wife Sylvia
get a position at Kaiser Medical Center and together they host
a small Bible study group for their church, Butler Avenue
Mennonite church, where Eddie was baptized and they are
members. Eddie is learning to be a good father to his daughter and two sons as well as a supportive husband to his wife.
Senior Hope Now staff and local pastors provide personal counseling to help Eddie and the rest of our street staff create and
enjoy a Christian family.

We estimate that each gang young man we help positively
affects the lives of six other people, including siblings, children and even parents. Sylvia's brother, who respects Eddie,
was influenced to pursue a good future by joining the United
States Army. A gang member named Yer left the streets for a
job in 2001 and sincerely followed the Lord. Consequently,
his two younger brothers have stayed out of trouble and also
given their hearts to Jesus. Struggling to control his anger,
another youth got into three fights at his first job. Today, however, Lionel and his wife are raising four children to know the

Lord who healed him. Lionel's transformation meant that his cousin also succeeded in our program. Few gang members or drug dealers want family members, particularly their little brothers or children, to turn out like them. Unless they change, however, there is little hope for those who follow.

The lack of protection from a responsible and dependable father often has devastating consequences for children. Predators, both male and female, have free reign to molest or rape both girls and boys. This abuse has devastating consequences, including full-blown alcoholism by the age of eight and distrust of a mother who doesn't believe you. The damage to self-worth is inestimable and seemingly insurmountable. Many times, because the subject is considered "taboo," the counseling and comfort that might provide some relief remains untapped. Hope Now aims to produce supportive, protective and educated husbands and fathers for the families of our cities.

Not as many youth as we would like choose to return to school. Vocational Placement Counselor Jesse Castro spoke eloquently for all of them upon receiving a college scholarship from the Woodward Park Rotary Club, "When I was younger, I was too ignorant to know I needed an education!" All street staff are also offered scholarships to attend college through our regular budget. Additionally, Hope Now has established a scholarship fund at the State Center Community College Foundation to encourage our youth to go to college. In 2002 we had 10 Hope Now scholars. While working as a camera operator for KGPE-TV, Tip graduated with a degree in communications from California State University, Fresno. But for many youth, school is an arena of failure they are afraid to reenter.

Peter grew up in a home where he was always told he would be a failure, so he didn't disappoint his drug-infested, dysfunctional family. A ninth grade dropout, Peter joined a gang so he could succeed at something, namely, crime. He also was a success at going to jail and, finally, to prison. After being released, Peter learned something about himself that changed the direction of his life. At his first Hope Now job in 1998, Peter discovered, for the first time, that he could succeed at something good, namely, a job. After succeeding at several jobs, Peter began to believe that he could have better jobs by learning to read and succeeding at school. So mornings and evenings he is attending the Cesar Chavez Adult School to prepare for the G.E.D. exams.

At a Valentine's Banquet, my wife and I sat with Gabriel and his wife who were both moving toward high school graduation in June. The following Christmas we listened to Platoon Leader Gabriel tell us about being a parachute rigger in the United States Army. God is using Gabriel's time in the armed forces to build a man of character. He was on his second time of reading through the Bible. Seeing Gabriel now living with vision and purpose motivated his older brother Reuben to go to adult school and earn a high school diploma. As the years progress we fully expect more of our stabilized and vocationally successful young men, most of whom are currently high school dropouts, to reenter school with a belief that they can succeed.

Almost 50 of our couples have gotten married, which adds greatly to the stability of the family unit. Once economic stability is achieved, marriage becomes a viable option. Because a man is providing for his family, his marriage has the possibility of being sustained. A newlywed talked about the effect of marriage on his home: "We still fight, but we don't threaten to leave each other any more." The stability of marriage and low housing costs have enabled ten of our couples to buy their own homes, which places them on the American economic escalator.

For the young men who succeed at various levels, we provide awards. The first award is a certificate received when a youth has completed all job preparation training and is ready for employment. This may be the first "diploma" a young man has ever received! At our annual banquet of 700 supporters, community leaders, employers and working youth, we recognize those men who have worked for one year, and for five years. At our 2002 banquet, 40 youth were awarded a framed certificate and a Bible for successfully working for one year and 18 youth received engraved watches for working five years.

Since 2000, Hope Now staff has chosen one Youth of the Year. This award recognizes the man who has not only done well at work, but has also made progress educationally, spiritually, and as a responsible leader in his family. We are able to evaluate his growth as he maintains contact with the staff and participates in Hope Now special events. Our first recipient was Tony of Sanger who has worked at Adco Manufacturing since 1998, married the mother of his children, and graduated from a computer technician course. Tony is currently enrolled at Fresno City College and is leading his family in regular church participation. I met Tony in 1996 on his first odd job while being supervised by Senior Vocational Placement Counselor Robert Rubio. Once given a chance at life, Tony even befriended and worked alongside rival gang members, some of whom were previously trying to kill shotgun-toting Tony.

Employers also recognize excellence. Albert was the first youth chosen as Employee of the Month by a Hope Now employer. Paul Evert's RV Country honored him by placing his name on the nearest parking space. Businesses promote leaders. "Not bad for someone with an 8th grade education," Kou thought when he was offered an Assistant Manager position at McDonald's, making $26,000 per year. Only four years earlier, Kou was a gang member with no direction to follow. Then Senior Vocational Placement Counselor Pe Maokosy began working with him. While employed for three years at McDonald's, Kou got his driver's license and obtained his G.E.D. He was such a good worker that he paved the way for other youth to be employed at his restaurant. Grateful for the excellent training given him by McDonald's, but not wanting to "flip burgers for the rest of my life," Kou became Assistant Manager at Kragen Auto Parts and is taking a sales and marketing course.

Sometimes the rewards of employment, although intan-

gible, are also valuable, as illustrated by the following from a
letter I received from Dr. Harold Hanson, retired medical
missionary of the Presbyterian Church U.S.A.:

> *On Wednesday evening, October 10th, at 6:30*
> *pm, Channy S_____, our long time*
> *employee and a refugee from Laos, locked the doors*
> *of our final shipment: two 20-foot containers*
> *totally packed with valuable and useable medical*
> *supplies and equipment.*

Channy and Jimmy had worked for almost two years helping the doctor send supplies to various countries, including
their homeland of Laos. Even the press and government of
Laos had recognized the efforts of Dr. Hanson's team. To earn
money legitimately instead of committing crimes, while helping their own people — I'd say it doesn't get much better
than that!

When a youth comes to our program, his counselor shares
his own story of coming up from the streets and how the Lord
helped him. In Bible studies each youth hears of God's great
love for him. After being cared for and helped in numerous
ways in the name of Jesus, after giving thanks in prayer with
our Executive Associate for getting a job, after experiencing
the change in worth and dignity that comes from earning clean
money, a young man often opens his heart to the good news
of salvation.

# CHAPTER 10

# Rescue 911

*Hope Now For Youth is a Christian emergency rescue team for young men, ages 16 to 24, who are gang members, have criminal records or are school dropouts. Through caring and helping relationships and employment, we aim to lift gang members from the streets to the American mainstream. We are motivated by our Lord Jesus Christ's concern for the poor, the fatherless and those oppressed by violence. Through deed and word, we strive to present Jesus Christ as the hope for life and life eternal, Almighty God as the heavenly Father who cares even more than we do, and the Church as the loving family that will never abandon them. Like our Lord, however, we will not allow fulfillment of our spiritual hopes for these young men to become a condition of our help. To fall short of providing loving encouragement and gainful employment for any young man who sincerely desires our assistance in leaving the streets is to consign him to prison or death. God helping us, we will not fail to always offer life.*

Hope Now Purpose Statement

As a young man attending church, I heard about "rice Christians" in China. Spoken of exclusively in pejorative terms, rice Christians were those starving Chinese who would come to the missionaries for food and, eagerly or insincerely, stay to hear the gospel. The well-fed missionaries addressing well-fed congregations would imply that these Chinese who confessed Christ were suspect since they always came back for more rice. Now I realize that the missionaries were the ones who were suspect. Ambassadors of the narrow gospel of their times, they were blind to the need of the Chinese for self-support and self-respect. To rise above begging was essential for the Chinese, if they were to freely embrace Christianity. Similarly, to rise above stealing or selling drugs is pivotal for gang members. Otherwise, in both situations, I believe it would be unlikely to find any sincere Christians among them. Hungry people think about food, not God, and are desperate enough to do just about anything to get fed.

When asked about our Biblical model for ministry, I point to the Feeding of the Five Thousand (Matthew 14:13-21) by our Lord and the disciples. When the physical need of hunger arose among the crowd, Jesus did not say, "All those who believe in me, come forward for food distribution. Those of you who don't believe in me, go into town and buy your own food." Jesus fed them all, and continued to preach the Word to them. Those who believed were as welcome to eat as those who didn't. All were well fed.

The 2000 census showed that Fresno's population is 40% Hispanic, 37% non-Hispanic white, 11% Asian, 8% Black and 4% other. Gang members come to us in a religious array, too, that includes Catholics, Buddhists, Pentecostals, Animists and Muslims. We help them all equally to find employment and show each one the love of Christ.

Jesus loves them all and enlists us to do the same as disciples, as "learners." Most instructively for us, Jesus said to his disciples, *"You* give them something to eat!" Gang members have the physical need for survival, of having food, clothing and shelter. The gospel compels us not only to meet these needs but, better yet, to teach them how to meet their own needs. Once they are no longer hungry, once they have a place to sleep, once they no longer have the fear of being shot, once they have the dignity of supporting themselves and their families, then we have reached the midpoint of the Good News, that safe haven in the gospel. To push for decision before entering that sanctuary of freedom is to risk having them "accept Jesus" just to get a job, to become "job Christians" instead of believers. So we work, pray and wait for the right person and the right moment, as indicated by the Holy Spirit.

It is our joy to sit with a young man whose entire countenance has already been transformed by holding a job and ask him this question, "Do you know why Hope Now helps young men who are dropouts and have criminal records, young men like you?" If he answers, "Because you care," we reply, "But *why* do we care? Thousands don't." A few figure it out, but for most we have the privilege of repeating what they have already heard from their counselor, from the Bible studies, and from the classes: "We are so grateful for what Jesus has done for us that we want to show him our gratitude by helping you." The Holy Spirit clearly leads us to those he has prepared. A crisis can precipitate the opportunity for spiritual enlightenment or actual conversion. Sometimes a new experience of God's power does.

Many times God's invisible qualities have been comprehended by Hope Now youth through discovering the natural wonders he has made. For those who have never been to the mountains or the beach, the trips and campouts we provide are truly spiritual experiences. Joel napped as we drove to Sequoia National Park and thought he was dreaming when he woke up and saw the tall pines. In his 19 years, Joel had never been in the mountains and was absolutely stunned by the size of the trees. We told him that every tree points to its maker. Upon seeing the snowcapped peaks, he said with a sense of awe, "What God makes in the mountains is really beautiful; what man makes in the city is really ugly." Joel's concept of the world would never be the same because his walls of possibility were being pushed further apart. The heavens do indeed tell of the glory of God and the earth reveals his creative power.

When we stopped at Pear Lake, Joel disappeared. The next time we saw him, he had jumped into the lake with all his clothes on, swum to a rock, and was standing proudly on top as the ruler of it all, waving his soaked shirt. A new concept of God grew that day in Joel. He also discovered a whole wide world outside of his mean streets. Maybe he could hope for more, maybe there was more to hope for. Almost every time Training Director Bob Pankratz takes Hope Now men and their families to a beach campout, only three hours away by car, at least one adult in the group has never been to the ocean or been only once before. Can you imagine what seeing pounding surf bordering endless water does to your mental and spiritual horizons? A trip to Yosemite National Park to climb Half Dome is like riding Apollo to the moon!

Overall, about 25% have responded to the gospel by giving their hearts to follow Jesus. But the other 75% will never forget that they came to a church honoring Jesus Christ, where the people of the Lord offered hope and help, even healing. Jesus still smiles upon them and us and he is not finished with either of us. The truths they have learned and seen lived out before them may yet lead to knowing the Lord. Ephesians 4:28 succinctly describes the process we have taken them through: *"If you are a thief, stop stealing. Begin using your hands for honest work, and then give generously to others in need."* First, they practice legality: stop committing crimes. Next, they practice morality: support yourself and your family with honest work. Finally, they are challenged to practice Christianity: help those even worse off than you are. If a youth only achieves legality and morality, he is a great success in our program. If he becomes a Christian, he is also our brother in the faith.

Commitment to Christ is an important step we hope every youth makes. Once made, however, the ladder of discipleship is very difficult for these youth to climb. To become a disciple, a person has to regularly be with one who can disciple him. There's the rub. The gang lifestyle is anything but regular. You go to bed when you want and get up when you want. Most days are not planned, they just happen. If someone says, "Let's go stealing," that's what you do. Primarily you just hang out, party, drink and do drugs. There are no schedules or deadlines. This reactive lifestyle is further a reflection of their families of origin, where nothing is done according to a schedule with the possible exception of attempting to get children to school. Hope Now has learned this the hard way. Given these circumstances, going to work at the same time five days a week is a miracle. Discipling, however, can easily become a frustrating exercise in random encounters.

We have tried weekly one-on-one Bible studies, only to find that there are more no-shows than meetings. When several couples had given their hearts to the Lord, we tried weekly evening Bible studies with childcare, even with dinner. After many telephone calls made and assurances of attendance given, our Training Director Bob Pankratz and his wife Kel would prepare spiritual and physical food, to have only one couple show up, arriving a half hour late. Sometimes they weren't even one of the five couples who said they would come! When another weekly Bible study for four couples became equally haphazard, Executive Associate John Raymond and his wife, Edith, opted for a once a month visit in the home of each of the couples.

If we are going to teach the Bible on a regular basis to our young men, we have to find them at some place where they regularly are. That place, amazingly enough, is at work. The Training Director now teaches, with the assistance of the counselors, lunch hour Bible studies for groups of youth working at the same location and having the same lunch hour. Each week interested men from Derrel's Mini Storage, WeatherTec, Di-Pro, and Storage Systems meet at a nearby fast food restaurant for a free lunch and a half hour of reflecting on spiritual matters. That's the best we've come up with but it's better than nothing.

In addition to teaching at family campouts and youth beach trips, we provide spiritual input at Hope Now Family Dinners. From an ambitious schedule of monthly dinners, we have settled on the only two that are well attended, at Thanksgiving and at Christmas. Preparing for 80 who said they would come, when only four showed up, quickly propelled us up the learning curve. As with other get-togethers we have tried, scheduling these dinners on a *regular* basis, turned out to be unproductive. Giving out turkeys and coupons for Christmas trees at Thanksgiving and handmade quilts and toys at Christmas certainly helps attendance at these dinners. The goal of these occasions is to meet the families, provide joyful social relationships in the house of the Lord, and proclaim the gospel. Once again, for each event, flyers are sent out, many phone calls are made and commitments obtained, but it's anybody's guess as to how many will attend. So we aim to have food left over to help fill their empty refrigerators. The most successful family event, eliciting the greatest response, may well be the Three-on-Three Basketball Tournament and Family Barbecue held each summer.

One of our most effective spiritual events has been to join with World Impact, a national inner city ministry, in an annual Men's Conference. In 2001, we sent 26 youth and staff to The Oaks, World Impact's conference center in the high desert. Souk, whom Hope Now has placed successfully since 1997, is currently at Children's Hospital Central California. He said that at the conference he heard "God talking to me" for the first time. Joy, who became a Christian through Hope Now in 1996, went home from the conference and brought his brothers to his counselor, "to know the Lord."

Of course, the most effective spiritual development and discipleship will ultimately occur within the context of the local church. Again, because churches meet weekly, Hope Now youth and their families face obstacles to continuing their spiritual growth. Yet regular attendance is not the only problem. Another challenge is to keep at-risk young men and their families from attending at-risk churches. Left to themselves, if they do choose a church, they often find one that gives them a "high," that fits their addictive upbringings. But two hours of shouting and swaying on Sunday doesn't keep them from sniffing gasoline on Monday. Sixty minutes of hearing "God Can" shrieked from the pulpit on Sunday doesn't translate into "They Can" live the Christian life on Monday. Still, even when they attend a church that encourages Christian growth, there is often the socio-economic problem. I have brought youth to my middle and upper class, 99% white Presbyterian downtown church, but this is not where they will experience the encouragement and comfort of Christ by seeing others like themselves following Jesus.

Butler Avenue Mennonite Brethren Church, a parish that decided to stay in a changing neighborhood, has a critical mass of our staff and youth families attending and joining their membership. The socio-economic mix is there, from poor college students to new immigrants to business owners, from a Hispanic congregation to a Southeast Asian congregation to an English-speaking congregation. Our youth see people like themselves following Jesus and being challenged to live as Christians. Caring couples and individuals, following the model of Pastor Rod Suess, are reaching out and enfolding ex-gang members into Christ's fellowship.

Tom was born an unwanted child who ended up in the foster care system before he was two years old. Rejected by his mother and never knowing his father, Tom grew up unwanted and isolated, fighting his way through school and eventually dropping out. Finding his only reliable friend to be alcohol, Tom eventually started living on the streets, hustling and doing whatever it took to survive. After numerous run-ins with the law, various incarcerations, and facing the prospect of another long lockup for forgery, God led Tom to Hope Now. He was 25 years old and had never held a job. Just prior to coming to Hope Now, Tom's deep anger surfaced in a drunken assault on a storeowner. Tom was placed on probation with an electronic monitor, a modern version of house arrest where every hour away from home has to be accounted for. Tom had a lot to be angry about. During our Anger Recognition and Release training, Tom gave his heart to the Lord and was discipled by Training Director Bob Pankratz. The Lord delivered Tom from both smoking and alcohol addictions.

After working steadily for four months and attending Butler Avenue Church with Bob, Tom asked to be baptized. Following instruction by Pastor Suess and three days of voluntary fasting, Tom presented himself on Independence Day, 1999 at the Fresno Pacific University pool to declare His faith in Jesus and receive baptism. There was only one problem —

an electronic monitor from probation on his ankle, which could not be removed or immersed! So Tom was baptized upside down. Four strong men, including Bob, carried him into the pool immersing him head down and feet up. Asked by a relative if he would go back to the streets once the monitor was removed, Tom replied, "Why would I trade Light for darkness?" The monitor was removed and today Tom is a full-time student at the university, working on campus, and living in an apartment where he can minister to others. Tom summed it all up this way, "I came to Hope Now to get a job and I got Jesus. Who would have imagined that?"

Early on Hope Now made a choice to be an emergency rescue team for gang members. Certainly we could have put more effort into fewer people, with some good results. But the right church can do that. Our call was to do what few churches could: to act as an ambulance service and emergency room for dying gang members. We are God's paramedics, picking up the broken from the streets and rushing them to help. We are God's ER team, stabilizing gang youth before they end up dead or in prison. Hope Now wants to reach as many as we can, as fast as we can, trusting that the neighborhood church will perform the functions of the acute hospital for sinners. We do this work for the Lord, but it is gratifying that Hope Now has received local, statewide and national recognition for its positive outcomes in the lives of gang youth.

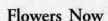 CHAPTER 11

# Flowers Now

*Please give me my flowers while I'm still alive.*
Lydia H. Minassian
The Author's Mother

One of the most pleasant surprises in directing Hope Now is discovering responsible adults who think we are doing something worthwhile and are not afraid to tell us so. It is also fantastically encouraging to have a board of directors who love me and tell me that Hope Now is doing what pleases God. Many times church pastors don't hear directly about the good they are doing. As a child, I used to hear from others that my dad was proud of me, but not often did I hear that affirmation from him. As a young man I confronted him and said, "Dad, I know you are proud of me, but it would be nice to hear it directly from you." Dad did his best to change, and I appreciated the effort. My mother is right: Flowers now!

Over the years we have obtained endorsement letters from the mayor, sheriff, chief of police, chief probation officer, and supervisor of youth authority parole as well as pastors and businessmen. A 1994 unsolicited letter and a 2001 Certificate of Appreciation from the Attorney General of California also added to our credibility as an organization worthy of support. Resolutions of recognition from local and state political leaders have helped introduce us to both the government and business communities.

Of course flowers are nicest when you don't have to ask for them. In the early years of struggle, it was very encouraging to receive a 1994 presentation from the Fresno County Delinquency Prevention Commission honoring Hope Now, "for outstanding contributions that go 'Beyond the Call of Duty' in helping the youth of Fresno County combat delinquent behavior. You have made Fresno County a better place for all of us." The financial gift that followed this presentation also helped Hope Now press on.

The City of Fresno presented me with the 1997 Dr. Martin Luther King Jr. Community Service Award "in recognition of your work in the Fresno community in keeping with the principles and values of Dr. Martin Luther King, Jr." Knowing the entire Hope Now staff earned this recognition, the award was still especially meaningful for me. Smart too late, I had only become an admirer of Dr. King at the end of his life. With accusations of being a communist swirling around him, Dr. King was scheduled to speak at the Second Baptist Church in Los Angeles. My wife and I decided to hear him for ourselves. That Sunday morning the sanctuary was so crowded that only when I leaned forward to peer around a corner could I see Dr. King preaching. My wife couldn't see him at all. But most importantly, we both heard him preach an amazingly incisive sermon on hope. From that day forward we knew that this controversial preacher was a man of God with a righteous call from the Lord. Three weeks later an assassin silenced his voice forever and we wept. I believe I am still influenced by that sermon.

In 1999 the San Joaquin Psychological Association presented me the 1999 Outstanding Citizen of the Year award for "contributions to the mental health of our community through Hope Now For Youth." Dr. David Bruce Rose, a licensed clinical psychologist who has donated services to Hope Now youth, was president of the association that year. This award, of course, was another honor acknowledging the work of my entire staff.

I first heard about the Samaritan Awards through a mailer in the summer of 1998. Entries were to be received by the American Compass of Atlanta, Georgia by August 26 of that year. Twelve finalists would be selected in September and ten prizewinners, including a first place winner, would be announced in November. So I entered Hope Now with a three-page application and waited ... and waited. November of 1998 came and left. Three months later, on Friday of President's Day weekend in 1999, I was informed that Hope Now was one of the 12 finalists and that a two-page form had to be filled out and delivered to their Atlanta office by the following Tuesday. That exciting news energized my hope and so I faxed the completed form and waited ... and waited. Heeding the Lord's gentle nudging and recalling my father's adamant organizational training, I made several phone calls to confirm receipt of each submittal and to see if we were still in the running. During this lengthy process, one of our submittals had gotten lost somewhere and needed to be replaced. Finally, all the wearisome and persistent waiting paid off. On September 14, 1999, we were thrilled to be notified that Hope Now had been chosen as the First Place Winner.

With the award letter, we received $15,000 for being "the nation's most effective and innovative local faith-based charity serving people in need." An elite panel of five judges, including former Drug Czar William Bennett of Empower America and Professor Marvin Olasky of the University of Texas at Austin, independently and unanimously chose Hope Now as the first place winner. The award letter defined an effective organization as "one that is innovative, a good steward with their resources, has a solid management team that demonstrates steady growth, teaches self-reliance vs. dependence, teaches their clients life skills, and lastly, incorporates a strong faith element to meet the spiritual needs thus effecting true life change."

Receiving The Excellence in Business Award and participating in the competition that selected Fresno as an All-America City were the honors Hope Now experienced during the following year. Development Director Carrie Good spearheaded our nominations. In May the 2000 Central California Excellence in Business Award for charitable organizations was given to Hope Now in recognition of "high ethical standards;

corporate success and growth; employee and customer service; and concern for the environment." The Fresno Bee sponsored the award in partnership with the Fresno Business Council as well as the Economic Development Corporations and Chambers of Commerce from around our valley.

The most exciting honor in 2000, requiring the greatest amount of effort, was helping to secure an All-America City designation for Fresno. Presented annually by the National Civic League, the All-America City Award recognizes "cities where citizen action has succeeded in making the community a better place to live." From all applicants nationwide, 30 are selected to attend a final competition where ten are designated as All-America Cities. Each city features three nonprofit organizations that have improved civic life. In 1999, Fresno had gone to the competition, but was not chosen as one of the final ten winners. Mayor Jim Patterson, who had consistently expressed his support for Hope Now since our inception, indicated that he wanted Hope Now to apply to be one of the three nonprofits for the 2000 competition. Following our presentation to a local committee, we were selected to go with two of the nonprofit organizations that competed in 1999.

After months of practice before mock judges, the All-America team flew to Louisville, Kentucky, in early June. The competition itself consisted of ten minutes for a presentation by the city, followed by ten minutes of questions from a panel of judges. Each team member had been preparing for certain questions we hoped the judges would ask. A video featuring the work of the three nonprofit organizations, interspersed with live statements at microphones, filled our ten-minute presentation. During the video, Senior Vocational Placement Counselor Pe Maokosy and Vocational Placement Counselor Eddie Ochoa identified themselves as former Fresno gang members. By the end of our presentation, our team knew we were making an impact as one of the judges was dabbing her eyes with a tissue.

During the judges' questioning, members of the Fresno team stepped to the microphone to address particular topics.

Finally, one judge asked, "I understand that you have a large Southeast Asian, including Hmong, population in your community. What do you do to include them in the activities you describe?" That was the question Pe, a Laotian, had been waiting for. Following an answer from a Hmong Explorer Scout, he stepped to the microphone with Eddie, a Hispanic, and said, "Hope Now For Youth has 33% Asians that we are working with." Putting his arm around Eddie, he continued, "See this gentleman here? Six and one half years ago on the streets, we would have tried to kill each other, but today we are brothers. I love this man." Following the gasp from our own team, we noticed the tissue box was now being passed to the other judges. Fresno was on its way to becoming a 2000 All-America City.

After our selection, Mayor Patterson said it was Hope Now that "put Fresno over the top" as a 2000 All-America City. Fresno had gone from being ranked No. 277 out of 277 most desirable cities in which to live to being among the Top Ten. From a record 97 murders in 1993, homicides had plummeted to a low of 27 in 1999. Auto thefts had dropped from 14,400 to 2,300. All this had occurred while our population increased by almost 25%. While grateful for the mayor's analysis and for public recognition of our hard work, we gave thanks in our hotel room to the Lord who made it all possible. God was lifting us up on eagle's wings.

On a windy November night in 2001, at the top of a hill in San Francisco, Hope Now was honored again, this time with a statewide award. Not having a tuxedo for the black tie banquet at the Fairmont Hotel, I wore my reverse collar, which is "black tie" dress for this clergyman. The purpose of the banquet was to honor five California nonprofit groups as winners of The Pacific Research Institute's 2001 Privatization Competition. The grand prizewinner was to be announced during the program. To initially qualify for the competition, organizations could not receive more than 25 percent of their funding from government sources. Our amount of governmental support that year was closer to 7 percent. That night

Dr. Henry Kissinger gave an insightful keynote address on a new world alignment, followed by a post 9/11 panel discussion chaired by another former Secretary of State, the Honorable George Schultz. Even before the banquet began, however, I wasn't the least bit anxious about what organization was going to win the grand prize.

When my wife and I arrived as requested a half-hour before the banquet, the Institute staff was preparing to take pictures of us with our award plaque. I noticed that our plaque had "Grand-Prize Winner" on it. Not wanting to jump too quickly to conclusions, I made an effort to look at another awardee's plaque to see if the wording was the same. Not finding the same wording on theirs, I asked our host, who answered my question by telling me to please look surprised during the banquet presentation. For $10,000, I decided that I could look absolutely startled! Once again each of the four judges, including Eloise Anderson, former director of the California State Human Services System, had independently chosen Hope Now as the applicant that best demonstrated the principles of innovation and initiative that the competition promotes. The 2001 competition recognized organizations that "embody the spirit of entrepreneurship, promote self-sufficiency, and increase opportunities for low-income individuals to pursue their American dream."

Considering all the wonderful recognition we have received, you would think that Hope Now For Youth is a vast organization with highly educated staff. But that is precisely what will *not* work. Gang youth have been hurt one at a time and they must be helped the same way by people who have been there. This is not rocket science. It doesn't require a doctoral degree, vast business expertise or sophisticated computer skills. I am still not a friend of the computer, but we have become acquaintances. In my spare time, I would much rather read than surf the Internet. Like many who are over 60, I find E-mail a necessary yet handy evil. It surpasses the fax for transmitting clean text, but I still prefer the more human contact of the telephone. Before web sites were so numerous, it used to impress some people that Hope Now had a web site. I was not among them.

This is not brain surgery; instead we are into heart transplants, and not just in gang members. Perhaps in these first few chapters God has changed your heart toward gang members. My prayer is that you now have hope concerning them. Maybe you have begun to envision the possibilities for them, for you, or even for your city? Hope Now, or a variation of Hope Now, developed to fit the needs of your city, could change the lives of hundreds, even thousands of gang members. Hope Now is the gift of God that can be offered to 1,000,000 gang members on 100,000 streets of 10,000 neighborhoods in 1,000 cities throughout America. Christian men and women of vision, passion and purpose will accomplish this, and Jesus will smile.

# Part Two

*What God Wants to
Do in Your City*

# CHAPTER 12

# We Could Do That Here

*Only in a dream world when you're out there trying to help the community would you think that there's going to be aid from somewhere. That's not going to happen. The bottom line is nobody cares. I went on Arsenio Hall and begged for some support; four people called us out of 50 million Americans who saw that show. I had to sit back and figure it out, why shouldn't people call? The first thing I came to realize is that the people who do care are broke. In order for you to care about a gang member, you have to have somebody that's involved in it. Then the other people are victims of gang violence and don't care about them. So the gang bangers' mentality is, "If you don't help us, we'll do this and that."*

Ice-T
*Uprising*

God always has ways that supercede anything we could dream of. He can make an individual care about the needs and hurts of his own people even if he's never suffered them. Although raised as an Egyptian prince, Moses was troubled by the slavery of his Hebrew people. God also can arouse concern in the human heart about people who are completely different, even about those who are feared or hated. A Jew honored among Jews, the Apostle Paul brought the gospel to non-Jews by entering their homes and eating with them, acts forbidden under Jewish law. Paul even befriended Romans, the despised rulers of the Jews. Similarly, God can use a person like me, who has no knowledge or experience of gang life, to care enough to change the future of gang members. He's done it once; why not again? Just because he did it once in a particular way in Fresno, however, does not mean that he will do it the same way in your city. But be assured, he wants to offer hope to the gang youth in your area. Here are the stages of development he led us through, as well as some of the things he taught us to avoid.

The passion and the vision start with prayer. Gather a group of Christian friends or fellow pastors and begin praying weekly for yourselves, your churches, and your city. Maybe you can take a day away to pray. Perhaps you will want to contact a local renewal group or the International Renewal Team (www.multnomah.edu) to lead you in a special prayer retreat. The Scriptures have several accounts of God giving a vision to those who are praying to him. Surely Ananias was praying when the Lord called to him in a vision, telling him to go and heal Saul's blindness. Saul was the last person Ananias wanted to meet, because this fierce defender of Judaism had been killing and imprisoning Christians. Fearing for his own life, Ananias protested to the Lord and reminded the Almighty that Saul was devastating the Church. Not one to be easily put off, the Lord responded, "Go and do what I say! Saul is my chosen instrument to carry my name before the world." How many chosen instruments of Jesus remain helpless and blind in the gangs of your city, unless *you* go?

In another vision revealed through prayer, the Apostle Peter was told, "Don't you dare call 'dirty' what God has declared to be clean!" Probation officers sometimes suffer the compassion fatigue that arises from always dealing with people at their worst. In a conversation with my mother, an officer was referring to his caseload as "slime balls" until my mother asked, "You mean those slime balls for whom Christ died?" Are gang members just rotten punks or are they precious souls waiting to be washed by the blood of the Lamb? It is these sorts of heart-transformations and mind-renewals that God wants to bring to Christian leaders through prayer. Prayer helps us think out of the box of this world and into the mind of God.

Once you have become earnest with others about prayer, gather as much information about gang activity in your city as possible, beginning with your law enforcement authorities. Realize that since law enforcement officers generally see people at their worst, they may draw a fairly hopeless picture of gang members. Also be aware that the primary function of law enforcement is suppression, not intervention. Peace officers aim to reduce gang activity by locking up the bad guys, a necessary but insufficient function of any civilized society. For unless someone intervenes, these "bad guys" will only be made worse by prison and will return to society as professional criminals. The unprecedented release of these felons has helped spark a rise in crime nationwide, first noticeable in Fresno during the last half of 2001.

To gain a more hopeful view of God's possibilities with gang members, contact an inner city church and see if there is an ex-gang member who would be willing to come with his pastor to meet your group and tell his story. Hopefully he'll feel free enough to answer your questions. You'll want to ask for someone who has been holding a job for at least a year and has left his old associates behind. Our experience is that some inner city churches or Christian organizations cater to the gang identity by allowing the baggy dress, using street names instead of given names, and not requiring a break with the old life. Just adding the name of Jesus to the Jewel Street Crips is not a prescription for change.

Ask a high school principal or vice principal to give you a perspective on the problem. Find out what the dropout rate is for each high school grade level. You'll probably be shocked. Ask what percentage of youth entering a high school graduate from that same high school. Why do kids drop out? What alternative education is offered to them? What is done to solve gang rivalries in school? What makes teaching more difficult today than 20 years ago? What percentage of kids has a biological father at home? At an open house, what percentage of parents shows up? Are there law enforcement officers assigned to campus? What is their function? Ask the question, "What are you doing to teach the artisans, those who learn by using a tool?" The tool of choice may be a violin or a snowboard, a

747 or an AK-47. A professional educator told me that 40% of the population are artisans. He estimated, however, that 80% of gang youth are in that category - artisans for whom the book-learning method of almost all schools is hopelessly irrelevant.

Try to find out what other churches or nonprofit organizations are doing to help inner city youth. Ask larger churches what inner city agencies they support. Can you meet the need by getting behind these or is there a specific need for the employment-oriented program of Hope Now? When I named Hope Now For Youth, I had no idea what other programs existed in our city. Only after confusion arose did I realize that six years before our founding, another local program had been started to work with at-risk and gang youth. They continue to do good work today as the House of Hope for Youth, primarily by keeping at-risk youth in school and empowering their families. Not surprisingly, once we even received a grant check intended for them. All people needed to hear were *hope for* and *youth* to be utterly confounded. Happily, as we became more known, the mix up lessened. Greater use of our trademarked name, "Hope Now," further differentiated our two programs. So determine early in your assessment of need if Hope Now will really add something unique to the mix of agencies working with at-risk youth in your city.

You may want to confer with someone in city or county government to ascertain what services they provide. Realize that few, if any, government programs provide long-term mentoring relationships with 24/7 access that gang youth so desperately need. Jobs are important, but a youth employment service is not enough. Jobs are important, but employment just for the summer won't solve your gang problem. Sending gang youth to apply for jobs open to clean cut kids is an exercise in rejection reinforcement. The 9 to 5 "social worker" model doesn't work with gang members. They have problems all night long and all year long. The "shepherd" model is closer to what they need. Sheep need constant attention to keep them from hurting themselves. They focus on the immediate and wander off. Unable to grasp the big picture, they get into big trouble over small stuff. The shepherd pursues them, even in the face of danger. Sheep will follow a Judas lamb to their deaths. Too many gang killings happen that way. Lost sheep need a shepherd to follow. They need to become able to follow the Good Shepherd.

A vital part of your learning process will come from reading other books about gang members. In addition to *Nobody's Children* (Valerie Bell, Word, 1989) and *There Are No Children Here* (Alex Kotlowitz, Anchor Books, 1991) already mentioned in Chapter 2, some books I found most helpful were:

*Do or Die,* Leon Bing, Harper Perennial, 1991

*Why L.A. Happened,* Haki R. Madhubuti et al, Third World Press, 1993

*FistStickKnifeGun,* Geoffrey Canada, Beacon Press, 1995

*Crews,* Maria Hinojosa, Harcourt Brace & Company, 1995

*Suburban Gangs,* Dan Korem, International Focus Press, 1994

*Monster,* Kody Scott, Penguin Books, 1993

*Barrio Gangs,* James Diego Vigil, University of Texas Press, Austin, 1988

*All God's Children,* Fox Butterfield, Avon Books, 1995

*Teenage Wasteland,* Donna Gaines, Harper Collins, 1990

*Peace in the Streets,* Arturo Hernandez, Child Welfare League of America, 1998

*When the Bough Breaks,* Sylvia Ann Hewett, Harper Perennial, 1991

*Gangsta in the House,* Mike Knox, Momentum Books Ltd., 1995

*Fatherless America,* David Blankenhorn, Basic
Books, 1995.

If you have an interested group, perhaps you can assign
out a book to each member, to read and report. Expect that
the language in some books may be cruder than you would
like, but that's the price of getting it straight from those who
are hurting.

Pray together over all the information you receive. Ask
Jesus, "Lord, what do you want *me* to do?" Although it takes a
large group of "us" to make Hope Now successful, it takes
only one "me" to be the spark plug. The issue is, "Do you
have the passion and the vision to make Hope Now a reality
in your city?" Do you believe, as I do, that Winston Churchill
was absolutely right in the shortest speech he ever gave: "Never,
never, never give up!" Is your heart broken over what you have
discovered about gang members? Is what you have found acceptable to you? Can you inspire a team of people to make
Hope Now happen? Can you make this ministry your primary avenue of Christian service at this time in your life? Is
your first agenda the welfare and transformation of gang young
men? Is the idea of Hope Now more an escape from a situation you must flee, or is it more a vision from the Lord that
you must achieve? What are your daily Scripture readings saying to you? Are Christian friends who know you well encouraging or discouraging you to pursue this calling?

Hope Now has had one sad experience with expansion.
Someone from a major California population area contacted
us through the Internet. He had money and contacts enough
to put together a luncheon of church and city leaders to hear
from our staff. But I had difficulty maintaining contact with
him. For a week at a time, I couldn't raise him by phone or e-
mail. Since we believed he was forming a new chapter of Hope
Now, our board of directors decided that I needed to be a
member of their newly forming board for at least the first
year. Unfortunately, what our board viewed as support appeared to him as interference. Consequently, because my in-

volvement was unacceptable to him, the idea of expansion to that city reached a dead end. In any expansion, there must be quality control from the home office. For any growing organization, this partnership is a common arrangement.

To succeed in this highly demanding venture, you will need to be deeply grounded in your personal discipleship with the Lord, have a clear understanding of your gifts and abilities, and be undivided in your conviction that building this all-encompassing ministry is God's foremost calling at this time. There's no way around it — spearheading this effort will require adding a volunteer half-time job to whatever else you are currently doing. Someone who has already experienced personal and vocational success, and who will make the time necessary to reach the goal, is required for this task. Do your children need you more at this time in their lives? Is your marriage strong enough to withstand the strain? Is your spouse as excited as you are about this commitment? How does your pastor respond to the idea of you leading this effort? Does he endorse your heading up a steering committee to bring this to fruition? Many questions need to be answered to determine if you are the right person with the right vision at the right time.

# Whose Vision Is This?

*In the last days, God said, I will pour out my Spirit upon all people. Your sons and daughters will prophesy, your young men will see visions, and your old men will dream dreams.*

Acts 2:17

God has given us the gift of imagination so that we can see visions and dream dreams. Too often we use this gift to worry about what evil might befall us, but this is not its primary purpose. Robert Kennedy made famous the saying, "Some people see things as they are and ask, 'Why?' I see things that are not and ask, 'Why not?'" Using our collective imagination, the board and staff of Hope Now prepared this Vision Statement:

> Obeying our Lord Jesus Christ, Hope Now for Youth envisions a safe, gang-free community in which all young men are offered a hope-filled future based on the opportunity to make good choices and to develop integrity by becoming responsible fathers who achieve their God-given potential in loving and supporting their families.

What is the vision you have for your city? Is it God's vision? From the beginning we were convinced that the idea for Hope Now For Youth was in the mind of God from all eternity. In 1992 he chose to reveal the vision to us. Write down the vision you believe God has for the gang members in your city. Even if only one person sees and acts upon the will of

God, a city can find new direction.

Begin sharing God's vision for your city with those necessary to put the organization together: attorneys, accountants and business owners. At the beginning I know that many thought the idea of Hope Now was foolishness, but no one could deny my enthusiasm. If you have the right vision, you will be excited. Discipline your imagination not to go into worry-drive. "Practical" people will ask, "Where will the money come from?" That's the wrong question to ask at this time, and it's never the primary question. The right vision from the Lord will attract the Lord's people to support it. If he is calling you to this ministry, be assured that our God has many others he will call to fulfill his vision.

Your credibility is always important, particularly since you are asking people to think out of the box. People are most likely to think out of the box when they are challenged to do so by someone who has already stepped out of the box. People can be stimulated to new thinking by hearing a gang member tell his story of transformation. It is difficult to mentally defend against a changed life. New thought patterns can also be generated when someone we respect challenges us to get out of our rut. My dad used to say, "A rut is a grave without ends." Many good ideas have stumbled on deep ruts and then fallen into them. Most new ideas have been buried alive there.

If you don't know a Christian attorney, accountant or businessman, you probably know someone who does. If you convince your friend of your vision, working together you'll be able to persuade others. Be sure to refer any interested persons to our web site: **www.hopenow.org**. Ask every interested person to pray about God's vision for your city, and to seek direction for how to participate in that transformation. Tell them that you will get back to them in a week or so. If further interest is shown, request the 11-minute Employer Video from Hope Now that contains five brief stories of gang youth transformation.

Part of a vision for the transformation of gang members is experiencing a holy anger over the unfairness of life and the hopelessness of their situation. I will never forget when one of our city's Christian leaders, H. Spees, spoke at a luncheon about Octavio, an innocent victim killed by a stray bullet from a gang altercation. Octavio was H's neighbor. After telling us he cried with Octavio's family over their terrible loss, H smashed the podium with his fist and shouted, "THAT'S UNACCEPT-ABLE!" H has a holy anger that keeps him living downtown, and working in some of the toughest neighborhoods in Fresno. Do you have a holy anger over what's happening in *your* city? I believe that anger is the energy given by God to make right that which has gone wrong.

H couldn't bring Octavio back, but he could refer Octavio's brother Jaime to Hope Now, to offer Jaime a safe haven away from the streets. Jaime began with Hope Now in 1995 and has successfully held a job ever since. He also attended Fresno City College and earned a certificate in auto body repair. In 2001, his current employer honored him in its newsletter:

> Traveler's Body & Fender is involved with Hope Now For Youth, which is a ministry that helps gang members and at-risk youth obtain jobs and gets them going in the right direction. Jaime Delgado was involved in their program. He has been employed with Traveler's since 1999 as a Painter's Apprentice. His hobbies include the restoration of a 1967 Ford Mustang. Jaime has a four-year-old son named Jesse. He describes him as being playful, with big brown eyes and curly hair. Jaime preps our client's cars for painting. He said his favorite part of the job is seeing the finished product, and watching the taillights as the customers drive away. We appreciate Jaime's wonderful disposition and his dedication to Traveler's Body & Fender. He has been a real asset to our team. Thank you, Jaime. Keep up the good work!

What Jaime has done with his life is not only acceptable, it's glorious!

Take every opportunity offered to speak to groups about the glorious vision of what can be. Generate additional opportunities. Ask to speak to church groups, including women's associations and adult Sunday School classes. Service clubs are always looking for programs. Present the facts you have learned about gang members in your city, to "open the eyes of the blind," and then offer the possibilities of Hope Now. Share the story of one or two gang members you have learned about, using pseudonyms to protect their confidentiality. Open people's hearts to the "other America."

For some listeners the most significant part of the vision will be the hope of reducing crime and violence. Others will be attracted to helping young people, and still others to the opportunity to present a holistic gospel. It matters little by which door they enter into the room of despair, as long as they see things from the inside for the first time. Here are some glimpses of the vision we presented and still present in Fresno:

- Help one good car thief get off the streets and 200 cars a year won't be stolen.
- It costs Hope Now $5,000 to permanently change the life of one gang member, but costs taxpayers $50,000 per year to adjudicate and incarcerate him, only to make him worse.
- If no one ever cares about you, you grow up not caring about yourself. And if you don't care about your own life, you certainly don't care about the life or property of another.
- Gang violence is the corporate outworking of the brutality inflicted upon its individual members when they were children.
- If we only do what we have always done, we will only get what we have already got.
- You would be hard pressed to find one person

on death row who has not been abused as a child.

- To enjoy family affection and caring, to succeed at something and be praised for it, and to receive economic reward for effort are normal human desires met illegitimately by gangs.

- A gang is an economic enterprise making money for its poor members; a job is the only legitimate economic alternative

- You can't live a legal life unless you can earn legal money.

- Over 80% of Hope Now youth succeed at holding a job and only 8% reenter the justice system, usually on a violation of parole or probation.

- How many of you would be here today without a job or the benefits of a job, including investments and Social Security? Your presence here demonstrates the importance of a job.

- If you don't believe you have a good future, you don't mind engaging in future-wrecking behavior.

- Every gang member is but a hurting child in an adult body, crying out for someone to love him.

- Gang members need to be taught how to stop being solely reactive, letting life happen to them, and to begin being deliberately proactive, making life happen for them.

- Many businesses have tried to help at-risk youth, only to be "burned," because the young men had no ongoing support and training structure like Hope Now.

- Given little significance by the important people in their lives, gang youth need attentive adults whom they respect to place value upon them.

- The 21st century's bottom-line must include opening the door for the poor from dependency on support from business taxes to productive citizenship as consumers of business products and services.

- Most school dropouts are artisans who can excel with a tool in their hands, be it a mammoth 747 or a deadly AK-47, a surgeon's scalpel or a killer's knife.

Your words and enthusiasm will paint images on the walls of the listener's mind, creating a vision of hope where there was none.

The first major test of the effectiveness of the vision you have cast is to find a Christian attorney who will donate legal services and a Christian accountant who will contribute tax and accounting services. If you have cast your vision wide enough, this should not be an insurmountable task. Many attorneys donate pro bono services to individuals and organizations. Accountants, to a lesser degree, do the same. A pastor who has embraced your vision may be able to lead you to helpful and qualified professionals. Once you have found these two key corporate resources, you are ready to contact Hope Now for general guidance on establishing a nonprofit corporation in your particular state. State laws govern the establishment of a nonprofit corporation. Here is where you will need to assemble a Board of Directors; ask your attorney to prepare articles of incorporation and initial minutes of the board, as necessary, and also have your accountant apply for federal and state tax-exempt status. Gathering a board of Christians who share the vision is the most important foundational step.

# CHAPTER 14

# Bringing Aboard a Board

*Never mistake motion for action.*
Ernest Hemmingway(1899-1961)

"Marry the right person. This one decision will determine 90% of your happiness or misery," reads the sign on my family room wall. The same could be said about choosing the right members for your board of directors. Board members in churches and Christian nonprofit organizations are often chosen for the wrong reasons: popularity, wealth, or prestige in the parish or community. Certainly you want to choose born-again Christians who have a long history of serving the Lord through the Church. We currently operate with a board of seven directors. Since board members are volunteers, not employees, Hope Now can require them to certify their agreement with our statement of faith *before* they are nominated for election.

## HOPE NOW FOR YOUTH STATEMENT OF FAITH

1.  I believe in the existence of one, only, living and true God, who is the creator, preserver, and governor of the universe.
2.  I believe that the one God exists in three persons: the Father, the Son, and the Holy Spirit.
3.  I believe that the Scriptures of the Old and New Testaments were given by inspiration of God, and are a revelation of His will for us, and the sufficient, and only, rule of faith and practice.

4.  I believe that humanity, in its natural state, is destitute of holiness, under the power of sin, and worthy of the wrath of God.

5.  I believe that the Lord Jesus Christ is the only Savior of sinners, and that by His perfect obedience, sufferings, and death, He made full atonement as the only sacrifice for sin, so that all who believe in Him will surely be saved.

6.  I believe that due to the pervasive sinfulness of every person, all must be regenerated by the power of the Holy Spirit in order to be saved.

7.  I believe that we are justified by the righteousness of Christ alone, through faith, and not by any deeds of our own; and that while good works are inseparable from a true and living faith, they can never be the meritorious ground of salvation before God.

8.  I believe that holiness of life, and love for God, for others, and for ourselves, are essential evidences of the Christian character, and that the only expression of sexual intimacy that is pleasing to God takes place within life-long heterosexual marriage.

9.  I believe that material abundance is a trust from the Lord, and that God wills to meet the needs of the poor through the generosity of His people.

10. I believe that Jesus Christ will come again, as the King rescuing His servant Church, and that God will create a new heaven and a new earth in which righteousness alone dwells.

11. I believe that there will be a resurrection of the dead and a day of judgment; and that the happiness of the righteous and the punishment of the wicked commence at death, and continue forever.

12. I believe that Christ appointed the preaching of the gospel for the conversion of the world and for the instruction of His people, and that it is the duty of His Church to carry into effect the Savior's command, *"Go into all the world, and preach the gospel"* (Mark 16:15).

Regrettably, a person can profess to believe all the right things and still lead the staff into an abyss of never-ending criticism and pettiness. To recruit helpful board members, measurable evidence of commitment to the ministry must be secured.

The second requirement for board members is that they buy into the vision, literally, by contributing $5,000 annually to Hope Now. Jesus said, *"Wherever your treasure is, there your heart and thoughts will also be"* (Luke 12:34). We want our board members to have their hearts breaking for, their thoughts working for, and their prayers persisting for the transformation of gang members. Making this level of financial commitment separates the superficial players from the serious investors. Most board members accomplish this level of support by personal donation. Some choose to achieve this goal by personal donation and in-kind services to Hope Now, or by personal donation and fundraising.

Incorporating a financial obligation for board members came from my 22 years as a parish pastor, where I observed that too often those giving the least financially, or none at all, made the most noise about how the budget was to be spent. Ironically, they certainly were talking about God's money, always about money I had donated, but rarely about any money they had given. Similarly, a board member who exhibits that nadir of rank hypocrisy will guarantee any Executive Director a miserable relationship with a board, for you will be serving two different gods. Furthermore, a board member who practices little financial support while offering profuse amounts of advice or criticism will undermine both the vision and purpose of the board. When it comes to board selection, I would reverse the rallying cry of an author of our liberty, "Representation without taxation is tyranny!" To build a visionary and effective board of directors, make sure that all members who speak about allocating resources are talking about God's money as well as their own money.

The next factor in choosing board members is the expertise they will bring to the table. As I describe our 2001-2002 board you will get some idea of the thought that goes into it.

Certainly other considerations could be made. I serve as president of the board since I was the co-founder of Hope Now. When another Executive Director takes my place, this arrangement may change. Vice President Bob Taylor is an entrepreneur with vast private business experience as well as service on other nonprofit boards. Treasurer Dale Garabedian is a Certified Public Accountant who donates tax accountancy services through Abaci & Garabedian. Necia Wollenman is the secretary and also a C.P.A. Involved with mentoring prisoners for years, Larry File also brings expertise from owning an insurance brokerage. Capt. Joe Cole, USN Ret., is involved in civic life in Sanger, CA, our satellite operation 20 miles away. By choosing to live in the downtown area, pediatrician Marty Martin referred Hope Now's first youth applicant to us in 1993 and provides emergency medical services as requested. Our counsel, Robyn Esraelian, has chosen to not be a member of the board so as to maintain necessary legal independence.

Both Necia Wollenman and Larry File became interested in Hope Now because they are personal supporters of our Executive Associate John Raymond. I first met Larry early one morning in front of my home, Hope Now headquarters, as I was returning from playing tennis. Demonstrating his great heart, Larry appeared to be very protective of his friend and pastor John and didn't want him to get into a bad situation. Since June of 1995, John has enjoyed doing the work of Hope Now even though it is "the hardest ministry I have ever done." As demonstrated by Necia's and Larry's outstanding commitment to Hope Now, one consideration in choosing board members may be their strong personal and financial support relationship with key staff.

The purpose of a board of directors is to set overall policies for the organization, not to get involved in the day-to-day operations of the program. This strategy presumes that the Executive Director is doing a competent job of management and administration. Policies set by the board cover personnel, drug use, conflict of interest, salary adjustment, sexual misconduct, scholarship awards, criminal offender record information, and working with minors. The board also approves a safety program and safety rules. Annually the board sets a budget and by doing so can approve the hiring of any additional staff. During 2001, for example, the board discussed a direct mail campaign, optical coverage for the staff, replenishing the Hope Now Scholarship Fund, an Executive Assistant position, a Job Developer position, City of Fresno social service funding, and the 2000-2001 audit. At each meeting reports are received from all management and development staff. The Hope Now Fresno board meets three times per year: in March following the annual fundraising banquet; in June for election of directors and officers as well as approval of the budget; and in October, which includes dinner with the staff. Board members serve one-year renewable terms. Board meetings are two hours long and are held from 4:00 to 6:00 pm of the chosen day at the corporate offices of Hope Now, my home.

Traditionally, one of the frustrations Executive Directors have with boards is based on the expectation that board members will go out and raise money to support most of the work. I have no such expectation; fundraising is primarily my responsibility, a portion of which is currently delegated to our Development Director. Senior staff members also raise personal support. A gift may come here or there because of the contacts a board member may have, but the legwork and paperwork are still the Executive Director's responsibility, not the board member's job. Likewise when it comes to developing jobs for our trained youth, that used to be mostly my responsibility, but now falls almost exclusively upon our Executive Associate John Raymond, assisted by Job Developer Marty Minasian. I still refer employment possibilities I garner as chief spokesman for Hope Now, just as I refer grant opportunities to our Development Director Carrie Good. But to start with, an Executive Director of a new chapter of Hope Now will be engaged heavily both in fundraising and job development.

Some boards of nonprofit organizations engage in

fundraising by sponsoring events such as golf tournaments, auctions and concerts. That may be an option in your city, although this was not an area I wanted to spend time developing. Being of the old school, I believe that God's work should be supported primarily by the freewill giving of his people. One fundraising possibility that I find to be a reasonable expectation for a board member is to require that each one buy, fill and host a table for the annual fundraising banquet.

There is a place in Hope Now for those who have prestige and success in the eyes of the community, who may or may not be Christians, and that is on the Advisory Council. The Advisory Council consists of those who are willing to lend their good names to Hope Now because they believe in what we are doing. The Fresno Advisory Council includes Mayor Alan Autry, Chief of Police Jerry Dyer, Retired Director of the California Department of Corrections Jim Rowland, and Teresa Davis, Supervising Parole Agent of the Central California Region of the California Youth Authority. Dr. Peter Mehas, Superintendent of the Fresno County Office of Education, and the Rev. G. L. Johnson, pastor of The Peoples Church, Fresno's largest congregation, also serve. Richard "Gus" Bonner, representing the Bonner Family Foundation, and Richard Johanson of the Fresno Business Council lend us their good names as well. William Haug, President and CEO of Children's Hospital Central California, represents the first major employer and one of the best continuing employers of our youth. Tal Cloud of Paper Pulp and Film and Larry Garabedian of Valley Truck Parts also were among the first to provide jobs for our trained youth. Kathy Bray of Denham Personnel Services, by virtue of her big heart and the nature of her business, has done the most to provide jobs on a continuing basis. By lending us their good names, attorney J. Wallace Upton and one of our recent employers, Rick Berry of Cal Custom Tile complete the Advisory Council.

In the early years, I scheduled annual meetings of the Advisory Council to familiarize them with our work, while urging them to also attend the annual banquet. I had hopes of them assisting the staff "in the areas of community relations, job development and funding." Certainly they have helped spread the good news about Hope Now, most make donations, and some have provided jobs. But I have come to realize that my Advisory Council consists of very busy people who earn their good names by dint of hard and effective work. Just to be able to list them on our stationary along with board members and key staff is of great help to Hope Now. I was to find, of course, that individual fundraising beyond their personal or business donations was just too much to expect. Raising the financial support for our staff was always going to be one of my primary responsibilities.

# CHAPTER 15

# If It's Green, It's God's

*Education costs money, but so does ignorance.*
Sir Moser Claus (b. 1922)

One secret to getting others to help you put together a faith-based gang intervention program is not being afraid to ask for all kinds of help. In October of 1992, I joined several Christian activists and other pastors on a trip to learn about the Pittsburgh Leadership Foundation and to attend the annual meeting of the Christian Community Development Association in Detroit. Above all else I learned that week is this statement from a development director at the Pittsburgh Leadership Foundation: *People of means are looking for people of vision to support.* What a freeing statement! No longer did I need to feel that I was going begging with hat in hand. I had a vision from the Lord to help the gang youth of our city and that same Lord had given others the means to help make that vision a reality. Many people, whether Christian or not, want to and have the ability to help at-risk youth in a variety of ways, but just don't know how to go about it. Hope Now provides them an opportunity to invest in a proven method of gang intervention. They are excited to see what their resources can accomplish on the streets of their city. Our Lord has planted these people in your city also.

The first major gift I received for Hope Now was from Harry and Zabelle Goorabian, parishioners from Pilgrim Armenian Congregational Church. Harry wasn't much of a churchgoer. He had a hardscrabble childhood and as a young man had played semi-professional baseball. Starting by selling World War II surplus parts out of the trunk of his car, Harry had made his money in nuts, bolts and washers. Now he wanted to help struggling young people. Zabelle had been in a women's Bible study I led for almost a decade, had become a devout Christian, and was excited that gang youth might hear the gospel. As the Goorabian's pastor for 12 years I had never asked them for money. In fact, as I think about it, in 22 years of parish ministry, I had probably not asked ten people for money, except on Stewardship Sunday, and that was from behind the apparent safety of the pulpit. Even today, after ten years of asking, I can't say I really enjoy it, but I certainly am thrilled about what their gifts can accomplish in the lives of gang youth.

Many Christian urban mission organizations require their staff to raise most or all of their own support. That has a chance of succeeding when a staff member has grown up in a prosperous extended family and been affiliated with a prosperous church. But since Hope Now's counselors come from poor families with poor relatives to boot, fundraising becomes infinitely more difficult. Having never been active in any church, furthermore, makes garnering support nearly impossible. It didn't take long for me to conclude that I couldn't ask the street staff to raise support. And I certainly didn't want them spending their time in multiple fundraisers when gang youth were dying. At the present time, we require management staff to raise the majority of their own support. What we will do when street staff achieve their bachelor degrees and have garnered the skill sets for management has yet to be determined. Experience has shown that we cannot support a professional position without that individual raising at least 50 percent of his or her own support.

When you ask people for a monetary or in-kind donation, you are helping them fulfill their desire to serve God, to assist the less fortunate, to be good citizens and to improve their community. I keep telling myself that the worst thing that can happen is that they say "No." Their "No" may feel like rejection, but don't be discouraged. There are many others who want to give and serve; you just need to find them. Begin with the people who know you and trust you. Think about all the people you know. Who could make a substantial donation to Hope Now? Who has a real heart for youth? Who has complained about crime and violence? Who is already giving to other causes? Those who have the gift of liberality will not limit it to Hope Now, and those who have the curse of stinginess will not refuse only Hope Now. Anyone you believe is capable of giving $1000 or more should receive a personal visit or, if they don't want a visit, at least a telephone call. Relying on a letter or e-mail to secure a major donation is a mistake, but leaving a simple brochure after a visit is good public relations. Once you specifically ask for and receive that first $1,000 or $5,000 gift, you'll believe in a God of miracles.

I have begun by writing about obtaining major gifts because it is much easier to get one $5,000 gift than one hundred $50 gifts. Make sure that before you ask you can assure the donor of tax deductibility and that you have your 501©(3) status at least provisionally approved by the Internal Revenue Service. The first Hope Now deposit on December 14, 1992 consisted of four gifts: $100, $800, $1000, and $5000. It is also much easier to obtain one $5,000 gift than to put on series of fundraisers that consume staff time and effort, which energy is better directed at the streets. In 1993 the principle of a youth earning his way to camp with sweat equity appeared to be sound, but holding car washes in 103-degree heat drained a lot of staff effort to make a paltry $300. There were certainly cooler ways of developing responsibility and relationships. Besides, people love to send kids to camp. Just ask them.

To gather a broad base of support, I speak at every venue I can. Over the years, this has included worship services, Sunday School classes, service clubs, professional groups, men's groups, women's groups, businesses, schools, colleges, radio, television and to newspaper reporters. Rotary, Lions, Kiwanis or Optimists are always looking for speakers at their weekly meetings. Contact pastors you know either in person or on the telephone and ask them to let you share your vision for Hope Now. Never use a letter, unless you want it ignored. Once I sent out almost 400 letters to all the churches in our metropolitan area volunteering our services and offering to speak. If you guessed "goose egg" for the number of responses I received, you're right. And I know the letters were delivered because I mailed one to myself. People today, particularly pastors, are so overworked and harassed, it's hard for new information to come to their notice.

To build Hope Now's donor base, I sent a letter, along with a self-addressed envelope, to friends and relatives telling them what God had called me to do and seeking their support. Once you have a donor, you want to keep them interested in the life transforming work you are doing. That's the purpose of the monthly newsletter printed on one page with your masthead above. Always include a self-addressed envelope with every newsletter to encourage easy response. I have yet to find it necessary to include a response form, as a donor's name and address are either on the check or the envelope. Only one donor has expressed her frustration with this fact, and she continued to give. We are not presently geared up for credit card giving, but may be in the near future. Then response forms will be a necessity. Here's a sample newsletter.

## APRIL NEWSLETTER
### 2002

### I'M NOT HERE FOR YOU GUYS TO GET ME A JOB

John Raymond teaches through the Gospels each week at our Thursday afternoon Bible study. The aim of these studies is to let the youth know that **God cares about them far more than we do, and forgives** the wild things they have done. Occasionally, a young man appears to indicate a genuine spiritual interest. Brandon had held a couple of jobs through Hope Now when *he came back the Thursday after 9/11, all shook up.* Doing his best to reassure Brandon, John was happy to give him the Bible he requested. In January of this year, Brandon panicked about making a probation appointment and quit his job without giving notice. This month, Brandon showed up again at Bible study and said he was sorry he messed up. *Because of what he had learned from the Bible, however, he had married the mother of his child.* He continued, "I'm not here for you guys to get me a job. *I'm here because I need God in my life.*" John was delighted to lead Brandon to the Lord following the study.

## YOU CAN'T UNDERSTAND HOW MUCH MY LIFE HAS CHANGED

Bob Pankratz has been teaching several lunch hour Bible studies each week, including one for the Hope Now youth at **Derrel's Mini Storage.** Last week Bee said, *"You can't understand how much my life has changed since God became part of my life. I have motivation, a better attitude and I believe I have a future."* We need God to make changes! Bob also conducts our Preplacement Interviews to certify that a youth is trained and ready to work. The two youth he interviewed one day both lost their fathers when they were six years old. *Angelo's dad was killed in an industrial accident, his mom is in prison, and he grew up in a home with no electricity or running water.* Though he had to do homework by candlelight, *he earned his diploma!* **Miguel's father was murdered, and many of his uncles are gang members who are either dead or in prison.** Both passed and are ready for job placement. "O Lord, may we (*you and Hope Now*) be your change agents!"

## MISSIONARIES TO CHINA REMEMBER GANG MEMBERS

This month we received *our first bequest*, from the estate of Rev. and Mrs. Verent Mills. The Mills were missionaries to China for over 50 years and were imprisoned for their faith. *Their legacy of Christian witness lives on through Hope Now.* In this, our tenth year, why not put Hope Now For Youth in *your* will?

## NEW EMPLOYERS GIVE YOUTH A CHANCE.

We are grateful to **People's Church** for employing John, Serey and Antione on their custodial staff. **Bledsoe Construction** has hired Henry and Xiong. After obtaining his Class A license, Casey has been employed as a driver by **OK Produce**. Monica is doing clerical work for **San Joaquin Pest Control**, and David is doing recycling with **Sunset Waste Paper**. **American AVK** has hired Julian to manufacture fire hydrants, and Jason is detailing cars for **Fresno Infinity**. How grateful we are to *all* our employers, new and continuing.

## THIS AND THAT

Many thanks for a grant from the **Gary and Barbara Marsella Family Foundation**. Your gifts are also needed at this time. I leave you with a "wisdom gem" from Orlando: *"You either live with the pain of discipline or the pain of regret."*

God bless, Your gifts are tax deductible.

I don't know about you, but I feel overwhelmed by any newsletter over one page long. My guess is that very few people read them, yet so many organizations produce them. If an article has appeared about us in the newspaper, I will put that on the reverse of that one page newsletter, but that's all I send out, with a return envelope, of course. People don't want scholarly articles about your work; they want to hear about lives changed.   Every few months I will recognize the businesses and organizations that have given us grants, and occasionally I will identify our new employers along with the first names of those they hired. I've learned not to place the amount of the grant in the newsletter. When people remember that you received a $1,000 gift and forget that you have a $10,000 monthly budget, they are tempted to believe that their giving is needed more elsewhere.

According to the 1998 report of the National Commission on Philanthropy, chaired by former Governor Lamar Alexander of Florida, Hope Now has all of the ten traits of effective programs to help people give better and smarter:

1. They are locally based and operated
2. They are entrepreneurial
3. They place strict demands on the people they help
4. The donors are deeply involved with the program
5. They stay focused
6. They depend on little or no government support
7. They measure their success in terms of improving individuals
8. Their goal is not simply to sustain people but to help them change so they can sustain themselves
9. They provide a refuge of tranquility, order and permanence in otherwise chaotic communities
10. Their purpose and achievements are readily perceived by anyone who visits them.

Among the *Guideposts for Better Individual and Institutional Giving,* the report lists:

1. Fund program operating expenses
2. Support the work of faith-based charities
3. Create economic opportunities
4. Stop drowning them in paperwork.

Some foundations we solicit for support appear to have gotten the message of these guideposts. Other funders, including state and federal government, want to invest in things, not people, or take delight in the paperwork. We try to avoid seeking grants that demand we hire additional staff to clear cut a forest to make reports.

The most likely organizations to give to your work are local foundations, churches and businesses. Our Development Director, Carrie Good, tenaciously pursues local banks, many of which make grants of $1000 to $3000, and local foundations, which make grants up to $5,000. She also writes letters of request to local outlets of national firms, which have given us from $3000 to $10,000. At the beginning, I wrote all of these letters and the requests have to be renewed annually. Churches, particularly of the kind or denomination of which

you are a member, will put Hope Now on their mission bud-
gets. You can discover what local foundations are in your area
from an established nonprofit, the library, the Internet or from
your regional foundation. Each foundation has restrictions as
to the type of funding they will provide, such as operating or
capital; the category of organization they will fund, such as
youth or the arts; and the geographic area they serve. Unless
they provide an application, grantors usually require a two to
three page letter describing the need that will be met, your
program strategy to meet that need, and the amount requested.
If you can't hand carry the application or letter, be sure to call
to insure that the fax, letter or e-mail got there. More times
than I can count, a crucial submission has not arrived.

Carefully evaluate any financial gift that is offered only
with strict limitations on its use. Some grantors will expect
you to start a new program with all or a portion of their grant.
If this stipulation will blur your focus, then just say no. I have
always been offended by grantors sitting in academia who pre-
sume that they know better what gang youth need than we
have discovered by working on the streets. One of their favorite academic exercises seems to be sponsoring a gang summit
or a conference of all those who are working with at-risk youth.
I have yet to see what these gatherings accomplish for any
gang member. Ironically, one major foundation says it is interested in violence prevention, but really wants to "prevent"
it by helping organizations provide healthcare since that's the
source of their money. Apparently, the dependency model of
the poor looking to organizations for foundation-subsidized
healthcare is more desirable than the self-sufficiency model of
enabling the poor to work for their own healthcare. The grants
you need are the ones that will support you in what you are
already doing.

A grantor who can see first-hand what you are accom-
plishing will usually support your vision. On a blistering summer day in Fresno, it was already 100 degrees outside. We
didn't know how many youth would show up for Training
Time in this heat, but over 20 did. Training Time is a weekly

diversity-training event, a chance for all races to meet each other as human beings needing a job. That day one of our grantors was doing a "site visit" to see Hope Now, one of several youth programs the grantor was supporting. While observing our program, the visitors heard from four youth already employed about what Hope Now meant to them. We often hear from working youth during Training Time, to give hope to the new men that employment really happens. Upon hearing these four stories of transformation, our visitors got misty-eyed and said, "This is the first time in our site visits we've seen kids." Remember, your letters of reference are written on the lives of the youth God has transformed. These undeniably positive, measurably significant changes in hardened young men are what inspire grantors and donors.

During the height of the dot.com fever, I suggested to my board that we go through the considerable effort of registering Hope Now with www.charitableway.com. I was naively optimistic that on-line giving might provide another stream of support for Hope Now. As a first step in opening this channel, I happily signed and mailed the Customer Service Agreement of July 2, 1999. Then there were the three pages for the Profile Web Page I eagerly filled out and faxed on July 7, 1999. On August 6, I expeditiously signed and mailed in the Addendum to Customer Service Agreement. Finally, confident of a great outpouring, I filled out and signed the new eleven-page Customer Service Agreement and Addendum. It was mailed on August 9, 1999. Ecstatic about our growing prospects for future support, I expectantly waited for newfound wealth from generous Internet entrepreneurs and a wave of web surfers to flow in. For all this enrichment of the Hope Now money market account, only a 9.9% service charge would be diverted from each donation.

On July 20, 2001, I was startled to receive a letter dated June 11 informing me that Charitableway, Inc., had ceased operations as of April 30, 2001. Being required to obtain two signatures so I could return the 2001 Annual Financial Report demanded by the Office of the Attorney General, California Department of Justice was another surprise. My surprise turned to chagrin when, considering the previous investment of hundreds of dollars of my time, I had to certify that Hope Now had received the princely sum of $18.02 of on-line giving. Remembering that half of that amount came from a merciful fraternity brother was even more disheartening. The expected financial river had dribbled in as two meager drops of $9.01 each, and now was completely dry. The lesson learned is don't put your hope in on-line giving, unless you can cause a well-publicized disaster while simultaneously offering to help rebuild. People still respond best to personal invitations to support local work, not to generalized solicitations.

The most effective fundraising tool for us has been the Annual Banquet, first held on February 10, 1994. Our program at First Baptist Church in front of 189 guests consisted of ex-gang youth telling their stories. The only time we had a speaker was in 1995 when we were fortunate enough to hear Dr. Anthony Campolo, Christian author and sociologist. That year banquet attendance jumped to 420. Each year since then we have had six to seven hundred people in attendance, hearing from the youth how God has transformed their lives through Hope Now. Current donors sponsor tables and invite potential supporters to sit with them. Businesses bring their supervisors and the Hope Now youth working for them.

Over the years the banquet has included various forms of special music, video stories of working youth, and Power Point presentations of youth receiving awards. But the most stirring portions of each banquet are seeing the youth themselves, many of whom still look like unfinished work, like gems being polished to a brilliant luster. Hearing them tell of the crooked alleys of their lost childhoods, the straight roads they are now walking, and the highways of the future they will speed down fills the banquet room with awe. The power of God is revealed. As the youth tell their stories, at first we hear the hopelessness of their former lives: "I started drinking heavily when I was 10, and took every drug imaginable by age 14... I can't count the number of cars I've stolen... My father will get out of prison soon... I thought I would be dead by now." But then we hear the hope they have now:

> Hope Now gave me a job, self-respect and a chance...
> The Hope Now family and my employer trusted me,
> even when I didn't know if I trusted myself... Hope
> Now not only got me a job. They encouraged me to
> stay in school where I graduated high school with a
> 3.0 average, and they helped me get my driver's license.

At the 2002 banquet we gave out 16 awards to youth who had worked five years and 40 awards to youth who had worked one year. When the youth and their families come forward to receive awards, the audience usually rises to offer spontaneous applause for them and for the Lord. Our guests see and hear what their investment and God's grace have accomplished and can still achieve.

The Chief of Police, the Sheriff, or the Mayor are invited to offer a prayer for the success of our youth, which helps youthful ex-criminals see law enforcement in a new light. At the conclusion of the program we ask for both financial and in-kind commitments, including jobs for Hope Now trained youth. Anywhere from 60 to 100 new donors make gifts or pledges, in addition to those made by current contributors.

Your city budget may be a source of funding but, as with all government grants, make sure they don't restrict your proclamation of the gospel or require you to hire people who are morally unfit for ministry. Never get to the point where more than 15% of your budget comes from government, because whatever government gives may be taken away the following year. All government funding is subject to the winds of political change, which can be very frustrating. You don't want to be forced to either hire or fire staff because of the fickleness of Caesar. Too much is invested in training good staff to let them go because of politics.

Once in a while you might come across special events that want to name Hope Now as the charity they would benefit. In 1997 America Sings was a July 4th outdoor spectacular that

benefited us and for a couple of years we were recipients of
donations from the Copper River Tennis Tournament. However, Hope Now has been careful not to become the benefi-
ciary of secular golf tournaments where sometimes the goal is
to end up drunk in the clubhouse. We cannot determine who
gives us money but Hope Now can decide which organizations wishing to publicly benefit Hope Now truly reflect the
positive values we uphold.

Prompt receipting of any gift is important to show that
the money is being put to use. When a charity takes a month
to acknowledge my gift, it looks to me like they don't need
my money or don't know what they are doing. If they are
disorganized in handling my money, how can they efficiently
run a program? We use a receipt letter, which gives us an opportunity to provide a little more general information about
gang youth to our donors. A return envelope is not included
with the receipt, as they will be receiving one each month
with the newsletter. I intentionally instituted this policy because of my being offended by receiving receipts for donations
to charitable organizations accompanied by further pleas and
return envelopes. Being asked for another gift while thanking
me for my last one seems to vitiate gratitude. We are very
grateful for all donors and hope they will give again. To keep
them thinking about Hope Now, all donors, as well as businesses employing our youth and interested government personnel, are placed on the newsletter mailing list. Assuming
you have been successful in raising up friends and funds for
Hope Now, the organization's bank account should be growing. Once you have some cash in the bank, it's time to think
about hiring staff.

# CHAPTER 16

## Raising Up a Bi-American Staff

*We all agree that your theory is crazy, but is it crazy enough?*

Niels Bohr (1885-1962)

When we started Hope Now, the only Christians I knew who had had any street experience were a few young men from at-risk backgrounds who were in Alpha Gamma Omega Fraternity. Although none had been gang member, I recruited staff from those friends I knew, my fraternity brothers in AGO. Adrian Reyes and Khetphet "KP" Phagnasay were college students who accepted this crazy challenge to have a part-time job reaching gang youth. As there was no African-American in AGO who needed this risky part-time job, I asked a pastor friend, the Rev. Paul Binion, to suggest someone. Quion Calip was his recommendation and became our choice to complete the original staff. Like the others, he was attending college and only wanted a part-time job. So we began on February 1, 1993 with a Mexican-American, Asian-American, and African-American street staff. Leading this bi-American team into uncharted territory was this Armenian-American, an Executive Director who knew little about the streets and less about creating a viable nonprofit organization.

Employing collegians turned out to have several advantages we discovered as we went along. To begin with, we could afford them. We certainly couldn't afford to employ trained social workers and, more importantly, the social worker model was not what gang youth needed. Gang young men don't have all their problems on Monday through Friday, from 9:00 a.m. to 5:00 p.m.

Not even most of their problems arise during business hours. Fortunately, however, college students are naturally up at all hours of the night, and don't mind giving out their home phone numbers. We have discovered that the staff's flexible schedule for availability is a crucial component for imparting caring to youth whose amorphous lifestyles require freeform time commitments. Secondly, college students are already in a learning mode. These counselors had very few preconceived ideas to unlearn, except the occasional conviction that all one had to do was present Jesus and then, without further effort or involvement, a gang member's problems would miraculously be solved. The enormity of the dysfunctions we encountered soon disabused us of that magical fantasy.

Finally, the most important advantage in hiring college students as Hope Now staff was their idealism and willingness to take risks. Very quickly we learned that gang youth might be threatened by our mainstream behavior. Adrian stopped his truck at the curb to recruit a new gang member and when he got out to talk to him, the youth showed him that he had a gun. From that incident, we learned to park at a distance and walk up to unknown young men. Another time KP was scoring baskets on some new kids at a park when one of them on the sidelines began to roll the barrel of his revolver. When asked if the gun was a toy, the kids began to laugh. This gave KP an opportunity to take the strong hint to "chill out." We learned to let unknown youth win. God protected us as we adjusted our ideas and behavior to accommodate the demeaning realities of growing up on the streets.

Originally, I thought the best idea was to base each ethnic collegian out of a church of their ethnicity. But when Hispanic Adrian began primarily recruiting Laotians in the neighborhood of his base church, Iglesia de Dios, the idea seemed less important. Then when we realized that the Laotian or Hispanic youth we were reaching did not understand the language of their culture, or the more formal language used in a worship service, matching ethnic counselors with ethnic churches seemed downright counterproductive. Over time we decided that the best base churches were English-speaking ones that cared about their neighborhoods.

When Adrian realized that many of the youth in the area of Iglesia de Dios were Laotian, he arranged a football game where our Laotian counselor, KP, could be introduced to the neighborhood. From that moment on, Adrian was accepted by the Laotian youth and, from that moment on, we began to understand a principle that is still true today: Some ethnicities need to see one of their own in leadership to feel comfortable. As long as Hope Now had a Laotian counselor, any member of the staff could work with a Laotian youth, regardless of the counselor's ethnicity. Our desire was just as strong to reach the more numerous and less assimilated Hmong youth, another Southeast Asian population, but for several years we could not find a suitable Hmong counselor. Prior to Yue Pheng Vang, a Hmong college student with a gang background, joining our staff in 1997, we had placed only one Hmong youth in a job. Since his coming, four counselors have placed 37 Hmong youth in employment, but with the lion's share still being helped by Pheng. Our current street staff consists of one Laotian, one Hmong and four Hispanics, two of whom speak Spanish. The few youth for whom Spanish is their language of fluency are assigned to these last two counselors. Having never been without Hispanic staff, we don't know if the same need for ethnic identification with a counselor is necessary for most Mexican-American youth, but I tend to doubt it. All of our counselors, of any ethnicity, have been able to help African-American, Mexican-American or Anglo-American gang youth, perhaps because these are the youth who are already assimilated to the diversity of the American culture.

As of 2002, four of our six street staff were gang members that we lifted from the streets, mainstreamed through employment and brought to know the Lord. Each member of our street staff feels called by Christ to attend college and to go back to the streets to help others who are where they were. All of these remarkable young men know both worlds, the streets and the mainstream, and can take others across that narrow bridge. As they do so, they share what Christ has done in their own lives and pray for the harvest.

*Who* these Vocational Placement Counselors are becoming is as important as what they are doing. Senior staff must never forget that these Christian young men are still at-risk of making bad decisions and may have generations of dysfunction to overcome. Since 1993, some staff counselors have had legal judgments served against them for bad debts or have filed for bankruptcy because they tried to use money to buy happiness. When you've been a "have-not" all your life, it's too tempting to become a "have" overnight, especially when credit is thrown at you. To buy a brand new car and add $3000 wheels on a college student's salary, even if your wife works, is not what most financial advisors would recommend. Racking up $10,000 in credit card debt, particularly while enrolled as a student, also would not be considered good stewardship. Other deficiencies of self-control have even longer lasting effects.

Because chastity before marriage and marriage before children have been untaught and unmodeled virtues, some single counselors have conceived children out of wedlock. By God's grace, each couple has married and are together parenting their child. Still, the marriages of the counselors are often rocky and relationships with their mothers and fathers are sometimes brutal or nonexistent. Yet these are the ones whom God has chosen for this work and even as we hold them accountable, we love them. Indeed, because we love them, we hold them responsible to uphold the standards of the Lord who rescued them. These special men are becoming the ethnic urban leaders for the church of tomorrow. The Lord is healing their brokenness; the generational cycles of satanic control are being smashed. So if you decide to commit to establishing this long-term ministry of life transformation, plan to be wounded with the counselors as well as hopeful for them.

Of necessity, Bible study and prayer are a significant part of the weekly staff meeting, because we know that God is the ultimate healer. Executive Associate John Raymond teaches from the whole breadth of Scripture the things that Christian leaders need to know. Lives are shared and prayers are offered for the youth and for each other. From the beginning of Hope Now, street staff soon learned to pray with sincerity that I am sure touches the throne of God. Over the years, we have slowly begun to observe not only knowledge of, but obedience to the Word of the Father. Like with the rest of us, the flames of crisis often motivate spiritual growth.

Whether I want to be or not, I am a father figure to the street staff as well as a boss. That role has a few advantages and some severe drawbacks. Out of frustration during one staff crisis, I penned the following.

## I AM NOT YOUR FATHER

I am not your father.
Please don't load me with his emotional baggage.
I am not your father.
Please don't confuse my authority with his.
I am not your father.
Please tell yourself this when you deal with me.
I am not your father.
Please give me a chance to be me.
I am not your father.
Please examine your response to me
in the light of this truth:
I am not your father.

I am your boss.
I hope I am your mentor.
I want to be your friend.
I know I am your brother.

As boss, I answer to God,
a Board of Directors, and the
community for your Christian
experience and ministry in Hope Now.
As mentor, I believe who you are becoming
is as important as what you are doing.
As friend, I hope we can share life together
someday when I am no longer
your boss or a father figure.

> Finally, as brother I stand with you
> on the level ground beneath the Cross.
> Jesus is all, our all in all.
>
> I am not your father,
> but in Jesus I would be honored
> to claim any of you as my son.

Each of our street staff appears to need a father figure better in some ways than the one he had, and I hope in some small ways I can be that. A counselor may harbor anger toward his biological father because the father abandoned him, let him run wild, disciplined him abusively, rarely spoke to him, solved problems violently, or abused drugs and alcohol. Any authority figure, and I definitely am a strong one, will feel some of that heat. Yet they desperately need to learn to trust some human authorities if they are ever going to deeply trust in God's authority, this God who is above all else, "Father." I have often wished I were a warm, gray-haired grandfather figure, but I am not. So I pray to be a faithful authority figure they can trust.

Each of our current street staff is either a first or second generation American. The culture clash is unavoidable when a young man grows up as an urbanized American teenager with school and girlfriend problems while his immigrant father still dreams of once again farming in the old country. In the Hmong culture, for example, a son went to work in the fields at the age of six and the families arranged his marriage. Many immigrants joined a gang for understanding, because "my parents don't understand what I am going through at all." By being the first in the family to speak English, the oldest son too often becomes the father figure and usually resents it.

They may have been in this country for generations, as have the African-Americans, but a fatherless gang member steeped in the ghetto mentality knows only how to exploit the "man," certainly not how to trust him. Where resources are scarce, everything becomes a "hustle" to survive, any way he can, doing whatever he has to. The drug dealer is one hustle, while the preacher, unfortunately, is perceived as another. Since no one was focusing on meeting his childhood needs, it is natural, although ultimately destructive of adult working relationships, to undermine and manipulate others to meet those needs. Taking the man out of the ghetto is one thing; taking the ghetto out of the man is wholly another. There are no quick or easy solutions to these problems.

Distrust between ethnicities or racial groups is pervasive, due to a lack of exposure to good role models of a different group. A gang member might have shot at someone from a different racial group, but he certainly never played basketball with him. It seems that everyone has to believe himself to be better than someone. Even I have to deal with racism in my own Caucasian heart, which erroneously thinks that our culture is superior when, in fact, only Christ and Christian values are the best. I must continually evaluate and gauge whether the way I manage and relate is just the white man's way or is actually the Christian way.

Prior to employment by Hope Now, all of our street staff have viewed education as an area of failure. Some may have dropped out in high school; others can't focus enough to succeed in college work. Even though we offer scholarships to cover tuition and books at our city and state colleges, it takes time for them to set goals and gain the belief that they can be academically successful. All of them are bright enough, but may lack study skills or the ability to perform under the stress of family or financial problems. It takes time to overcome the prophecies of failure given them by a parent. One motivator toward educational achievement, however, appears to be having the responsibility to support a child.

When compared to the mainstream, the street staff also appears to have more crises that diffuse their focus. They may be distracted by living with one's dysfunctional parents, rearing abandoned younger siblings, facing a divorce, or fighting for a brother who is sentenced to life in prison without possibility of parole. Vocational Placement Counselor Sergio Perez, Jr., with a young wife and two small children, has had to take his teenage brother and sister to live in his already overcrowded apartment. In addition to trying to grow his own marriage and working, Sergio is supposed to cope with raising two teenagers. I can hardly imagine the superhuman effort Sergio must make to pass his college courses. By the grace of God, he is doing an admirable job, but I'm overwhelmed just thinking of what Sergio is attempting. As difficult as transforming gang youth can be, our work may be the most predictable part of Sergio's life.

For the first three years, we tried as much as possible to provide direct supervision for the street staff. In 1996, the most senior Vocational Placement Counselor Alex Arellano became Program Coordinator, but we soon discovered that it is difficult to supervise a growing staff that is classified by worker's compensation as "outside sales." Much of our street staff's work is conducted outside of their offices, and even those offices are located all over the city. Consequently, for the next five years, I coped with the situation by employing my usual management style, which is to outline the job, expect people to be self-initiating, give staff their head and receive reports of results. Fortunately, John Raymond provided some supervision of the street staff, which was really beyond his job description. In retrospect I realize that I did not provide sufficient staff development and guidance to achieve maximum potential, and after a while the street staff was telling me so. By bringing aboard Operations Manager Joan Minasian, with experience as a Vice President of the American Cancer Society, we plan to rectify the situation.

Until June of 1995, when John Raymond was hired, I was the only senior staff. As Hope Now grew, we added a part-time Development Director, Kaye Cummings, in May of 1996. Bob Pankratz joined us in April of 1998 and is our Training Director today. With the resignation of Kaye in May of 1999, we hired Carrie Good as Development Director and she became full-time in September of that year. During 2001, Joan Minasian began working for us as part-time Operations Manager and Marty Minasian began as part-time Job Developer assisting John. The goal for 2002 is 137 successful first-time placements of gang youth in jobs, in addition to providing a corresponding number of subsequent placements for current Hope Now youth who have been laid off. More modest goals, of course, can be and have been achieved with less staff.

The current professional staff is all Caucasian, but the long-term goal is to train up the current street staff to graduate from college and to gain the necessary skill sets for professional positions, possibly with Hope Now. Once a counselor earns a four-year degree, there will be many doors of opportunity open to him. Adrian Reyes, one of our original counselors, was the first to reach that goal and is currently working as a Case Manager with disabled at-risk youth at the Central Valley Regional Center. For the financial health of Hope Now, all professional staff must be involved in personal fundraising to support their position. Since street staff are not required to do personal fundraising, a future challenge for senior staff will be to guide street staff to sources for personal fundraising once they are educationally and experientially qualified to move into professional positions with Hope Now.

In concert with the Operations Manager and the Training Director, each counselor sets goals for the year. The primary measure of success for a Vocational Placement Counselor is the number of successful placements of new youth he has trained into jobs. Success is measured by a youth working 30 days or longer. Additional goals may include leading one special event, such as a fishing trip, retreat, campout, or beach trip. With six lunch hour Bible studies at businesses, the Training Director is equipping each counselor to reach the goal of effectively leading one of these weekly studies.

But to begin a Hope Now ministry, I believe you could function with only two staff, one to work the community and the other to work the streets. I don't know if it is possible to operate Hope Now with just one staff person, but I would guess it could get pretty lonely and discouraging. To find in one person the mix of abilities required for public relations, fundraising, and job development, as well as gang member recruitment and mentoring, will be daunting. And when a youth breaks your heart or faces a seemingly insurmountable problem, who would encourage you to press on? When businesses won't listen to you because they don't yet believe these kids can be good employees, who would pray with you? Jesus sent his disciples out two-by-two into a hostile world. Prayerfully let God reveal the team he has chosen to work with you. Start however you can to train gang youth for life; many will eagerly grab the opportunity.

# CHAPTER 17

# Training Right from Wrong

*While we have foolishly invested our precious resources in a criminal justice approach to solving our crime problem we have nothing to show for it except poorer schools, poorer services for youth, and more people on the streets unemployable because they have a criminal record. We have a crisis of violent youth on our streets that we pretend can be solved by a strategy that has already failed.*

Geoffrey Canada
*Fist Stick Knife Gun*

Before you can train a gang youth, you have to gain his trust. A counselor has to take the time to build a caring and helping relationship that affirms a youth's abilities and convinces him that he can go through life the right way. We accomplish this by meeting with a youth, taking him out for lunch, working alongside him in an odd job, and helping him get his Social Security Card or California ID. Playing dominoes, chess, checkers, ping-pong or foosball gives the counselor an opportunity to laugh and play with the youth. Gang youth have far too little play in their lives. One-on-one training classes also build up that all-important trusting and affirming relationship.

By far, the best way to strengthen a relationship is to listen, to ask the right questions and to let a gang youth tell you who he is. A Hope Now counselor may be the first responsible person to listen to a young man's troubled story. Sometimes we need to assure them that nothing they say will shock us. The following are some of the questions we use.

# BUILDING RELATIONSHIPS WITH AT-RISK YOUTH

## QUESTIONS YOU MIGHT ASK

1. How did you hear about Hope Now?
2. What caused you to decide to call us?
3. Where have you worked before?
4. What job did you enjoy the most?
5. What kind of work do you enjoy doing?
6. If you could do anything you wanted to do, what would you do?
7. How long did you work at your job?
8. What happened that you are no longer working at that job?
9. Tell me a little about your education.  How far did you go in school?
10. What happened that you quit?
11. What did you like most about school? Least?
12. Do you have any dreams of ever going back?
13. Who are you living with?
14. Is it a good living situation or would you like to leave?
15. What can you tell me about your family?
    - -How many brothers/sisters do you have?
    - -Are they older or younger?
    - -Where do they live?
16. Tell me a little bit about your dad and mom?
    - -Do you have a good relationship with your dad and mom?
    - -Did both of your parents raise you?
    - -Do you have a step dad /step mom?
    - -Where is your mom? Does your mom work outside the home?
    - -Where is your dad?
    - -What does your dad do for a living?
17. What do you like or dislike about how you were raised?
18. Growing up, what would you have liked from them that you did not get?
19. Have you lived here all your life?
    - -Where else have you lived?
    - -Were you born in the United States?

20. Where have you been outside of the city?
21. Do you have a girlfriend?
    - What is her name?
    - How did you meet each other?
    - Are you living together?
    - Do you ever see yourself getting married?
22. Do you have any children?
    - What are their names?
    - How old are they?
    - How often do you see them? Do you get along with their mother?
    - Do you like being a dad?
    - What do you enjoy most about it?
    - What is the hardest thing about being a dad?
    - How many children would you like to have?
23. Did you ever get in trouble with the law?
    - How did that happen? What were you convicted of?
    - Did you have to serve time?
        - How long? Where?
        - When did you get out?
    - Are you or were you a gang member?
    - Are you on probation or parole?
    - For what charges?
    - When do you get off probation or parole?
    - Do you have any community service hours to complete?
    - Do you have any outstanding warrants?
24. Are you taking any medications? Are you under a doctor's care?
    - Are there any health problems that will prevent you from holding a job?
25. When was the last time you used illegal drugs?
26. Has God ever been a part of your life? How?
27. Did you have any kind of religious background?
    - Did you ever go to church/temple/mosque?
28. What do you think of this Jesus we talk about?
29. Is this something you are interested in talking about or are you not ready for that?

By using some of these questions and listening in an understanding way, a counselor builds a bridge into a young man's life. If a young man is offended by any of these questions, we explore why. Jesus said, " The truth shall set you free." If a young man is not ready to face the truth about himself, he's not ready for the kind of help we provide.

The most important training we give to gang youth is life skills training, particularly as they apply to holding a job. Christian values are woven throughout the classes we teach. The Vocational Placement Counselors are currently responsible for teaching three of the six job preparation classes, which enable them to intentionally spend one-on-one time with a youth. These classes are Job Success, Job Search, and Drug and Alcohol Awareness. Job Success covers the following areas:

- Work traits that help keep your job
- Work traits that can get you fired
- Acceptable and unacceptable reasons to miss work
- What to do if you are running late or are sick
- How to work with difficult people
- Reliable and unreliable sources of transportation
- Leaving or quitting a Hope Now job.

To inspire hope of job success, we show a videotape of five Hope Now youth who have found jobs. They see and hear young men just like them who have succeeded at holding jobs and supporting their families.

About 10% of our first-time youth find a job for themselves, either during or after training. Job Search teaches a youth how to look for work on his own by covering the following topics:

- Why are jobs always available?
- Determining your skills and strengths
- Methods of searching for a job
- Filling out an application
- How to get an interview
- Making a good impression at the interview

· Questions to expect during the interview

A professional videotape presentation of the dos and don'ts of interviewing is included in this class. A job application is filled out by each youth, which he keeps. This application, containing previous work history and references, will help the youth fill out the application required of him when he is placed in a job.

The third class taught by the Vocational Placement Counselors is the Drug and Alcohol Awareness Class. Through relating his own experiences, the counselor helps the youth understand the hazards of drug and alcohol use, as well as the signs of addiction. Many businesses require passing a drug test as a condition of employment. The counselor tells why he gave up using drugs and alcohol. Liver damage, memory loss, heart problems, depression, convulsions, and even death are some of the effects on the mind and body. Impaired eyesight, slower reaction time, lessened concentration and poor coordination or judgment due to abuse can cause work-related injuries. Most businesses will test the employee for substance abuse after an accident and, if the test is positive, will fire the youth and deny him any benefits. Addiction can also affect productivity, the quality of work, the ability to get along with others, and even the motivation to hold a job. Tragically, drug addiction may even encourage an employee to steal from his employer. Being absent on Mondays sometimes is a sign of an addiction, and usually is a sign of too much partying on the weekends.

The greatest problem we face in preparing drug-free employees is marijuana use, which appears to be as socially acceptable in their neighborhoods as drinking beer. Weed stays in body tissue the longest of the common illegal drugs, for up to four weeks, and is continually excreted in the urine. When a youth has last used pot is an important consideration in whether or not he is taken to a job. During the intake process, we require a youth to read, if possible, and agree to the following policy:

## ADDICTIONS, ABUSE AND TATTOO POLICY

### BACKGROUND

Tagging, the illegal use of any drug, including inhalants, or the excessive use of alcohol is unacceptable for anyone who desires a permanent job. All these habits temporarily relieve stress and give you the false impression that you are better than you are. The truth is these habits only add to your life problems. Too many Hope Now youth have held a permanent job and then lost it because of tagging, a DUI, or committing a crime while drunk or "high," most often spousal abuse. They started clean, but began tagging or abusing again. For taggers, tagging is an addiction and one of your drugs of choice.

Often a job includes operating machinery or using tools. When under the influence of alcohol or drugs, you are a danger to others and yourself. When abusing regularly, your personality changes for the worse, sporting an attitude that can get you fired. Tagging in restrooms or elsewhere can also get you fired.

Most employers consider visible tattoos as signs of the gang/street lifestyle that can cause problems in the workplace. It is already difficult enough for Hope Now to find jobs for those who have been gang members or taggers, have not graduated from high school or have earned a criminal record. Sporting visible tattoos makes job placement almost impossible.

### AGREEMENT

As a registered participant in the Hope Now For Youth program, as of today I will stop any tagging and use of illegal drugs, including marijuana or inhalants, and will not tag or abuse as long as I am in the program or in a job given me by Hope Now For Youth. I will also not abuse alcohol to get drunk at any time. If on probation or parole, I will not use any alcohol at all.

I will submit to any drug/inhalant/alcohol test or home/personal inspection for tagging given me by a staff member of

Hope Now For Youth. If I fail such test or inspection, I will enter a program for addicts approved by Hope Now. If I refuse a Hope Now test or inspection, or fail to attend an approved program, I will be removed from the Hope Now program and my Hope Now employer, if any, will be notified of my removal. If I get a new visible tattoo, I will be removed from the Hope Now program and my Hope Now employer, if any, will be notified of my removal.

I fully agree to the above terms of being a registered participant in the Hope Now For Youth program and I will hang out with friends who are working and not abusers/taggers/being tattooed. If I feel unable to keep these terms at this time, I must enter a program for addicts approved by Hope Now prior to being registered in the Hope Now program. Failure to stay in the program for addicts will be cause for denial of all Hope Now services. This agreement will remain in force until written notice of cancellation is given to Hope Now.

Signature:_____ Date:_____

Print Name:_____

Parent's Signature:_____ Date_____
(If Youth Under 18)

Witness Signature:_____ Date_____

Before we take a youth to a job, we ask again about the last time he used drugs. If we are not sure about him being clean from drugs and still wish to take him to a job, we may administer our own drug test. A youth may claim he tested positive for marijuana by being in the same room with someone else who was smoking weed. However, according to the drug testing experts and to our own knowledge of how and when people smoke pot, second-hand contamination is virtually impossible. To avoid drug detection, a youth may say he can't urinate, or try to dilute his sample with water, or even try to substitute someone else's urine for his own. He may even attempt to mask evidence of drug use with various home remedies or with advertised products having such outrageous names as Urine Luck. None of these ploys, however, will result in a clean drug test.

The Addictions Self Assessment Checklist we use was prepared by the Presbyterian Network on Alcohol & Other Drug Abuse and is available by calling (800)325-9133. A similar checklist obtained from your local Alcoholics Anonymous group might do just as well. Hope Now is not equipped to help true addicts become free of their addiction, but we do seem to help those who recreationally use drugs to get high or use alcohol to get drunk. Most Hope Now youth stop recreational drug use and many moderate their use of alcohol in favor of experiencing the dignity of holding a job and supporting a family. The youth we are unable to help because of addiction appear not to want to give up their dependency on mood-altering substances. Some work for two to three years, supporting their families, even buying homes, and then fall back under the full destructive power of their addiction. We still pray for them, hoping that they will enter a program and get help.

The last part of the Drug and Alcohol Addictions Awareness Class deals with ways to stay drug-free, the most important and probably most difficult of which is staying away from drug-using buddies. A job, positive things to do, family commitment, sober friends, the threat of being jailed on a violation of parole or probation and commitment to Christ can all help a young man in leading a sober life, *if he wants to stay clean*. But, we emphasize, there are only two things that can keep him off drugs: Himself and Death. Finally, to emphasize the gravity of his choices, we recount several stories of Hope Now youth who have died of a drug overdose or choked to death on their own vomit when passed out drunk. We grieve over such losses, but have learned from them. We've discovered that so much of substance abuse is but an anesthetic for the heart pain and uncontrollable anger arising from a lost childhood, a sorrow a youth is desperate to forget.

Violence and rage are "normal" in the families and neighborhoods gang youth inhabit. Anger Recognition and Release is both a psychological and spiritual presentation that I developed in 2000, and still teach, to help angry youth get a handle on what they call "stress." It encourages them to understand the sources of their anger and then to ask the Lord to take the rage from them. We begin by showing a videotaped portion of a Public Broadcasting Documentary entitled, *What Can We Do About Violence?* In it Bill Moyers asks young men locked up for murder in the California Youth Authority why they turned to violence. Their introspective and perceptive answers about their upbringing well describe the situations in which our young men grew up.

After our youth have heard others like themselves speak about the sources of the anger that leads to violence, we ask them to fill out the following assessment tool. I used to let them read it and fill it out, until I discovered that several of the youth were just going through the motions, too embarrassed to say they couldn't read well. Prior to reading the questions aloud to them, I explain that the most painful events of their lives have probably already happened, because children are most vulnerable to and least able to escape or control painful situations inflicted on them by adults.

## FAMILY VIOLENCE SELF-ASSESSMENT

### Physical Violence in Your Family

1. When you were bad, were you hit with anything but an open hand?                                                  Yes__ No__
2. Were you sexually molested by anyone?     Yes__ No__
3. Were you threatened with a weapon?       Yes__ No__
4. Were you given alcohol or drugs?          Yes__ No__
5. Were you beaten up by a family member?    Yes__ No__
6. Were objects thrown at you to hurt you?     Yes__ No__
7. Did anyone abuse anyone else in front of you?  Yes__ No__
8. Were you intentionally injured by an adult?    Yes__ No__

9.  Were you denied food, water, sleep or
    adequate clothing?                              Yes__  No__
10. Were you denied available medical care?         Yes__  No__
11. Did arguments get settled by fighting?          Yes__  No__

## Emotional Violence in Your Family

1.  Were you cursed and called names?               Yes__  No__
2.  Were you told you were stupid, dumb, or going
    to be a loser?                                  Yes__  No__
3.  Were you told or made to feel, "I wish you were
    never born?"                                    Yes__  No__
4.  Were you treated worse than your brothers
    and sisters?                                    Yes__  No__
5.  Were alcohol or illegal drugs used regularly
    in your family?                                 Yes__  No__
6.  Was there any other illegal activity, like prostitution  Yes__  No__
    or gambling, in your home?
7.  Was Mom or Dad or both not there for you?       Yes__  No__
8.  Were promises made but not kept?                Yes__  No__
9.  Do you have a learning disability?              Yes__  No__
10. Was a favorite toy or pet destroyed by a parent?  Yes__  No__
11. Did you have to be the parent?                  Yes__  No__
12. Were your parents too busy to hug and kiss
    you as a child?                                 Yes__  No__
13. Did your parents neglect to tell you,
    "I love you," often enough?                     Yes__  No__
14. Did your parents praise you too little?         Yes__  No__
15. Did your parents share their emotional or
    sexual problems with you?                       Yes__  No__
16. Were you ever locked up, tied up, locked out
    or lost by your family?                         Yes__  No__
17. Did your parent encourage you to engage in
    criminal activity?                              Yes__  No__
18. Was school so unimportant that you got no
    help from your family?                          Yes__  No__
19. Were you kept in the dark about important
    events that affected you?                       Yes__  No__
20. Were you lied to by your parents?               Yes__  No__

**Spiritual Violence in Your Family**

1. Did you witness or suffer satanic ritual abuse?          Yes__ No__
2. Did anyone in your family seek power from or
   worship Satan?                                          Yes__ No__
3. Have you taken part in any animal sacrifices?           Yes__ No__
4. Have you prayed to the spirits of the dead
   (ancestors)?                                            Yes__ No__
5. Did you witness or take part in any satanic rites?      Yes__ No__

The youth is then asked to total up the number of affirmative answers to the questions. Any score of 5 or more indicates growing up in a violent family. A few youth have scored as high as 23 on this evaluation; one smiling 17-year-old scored a record 24. Gang youth need to be assured that none of the behaviors described in this assessment is "normal" or acceptable. For many youth, this discussion is the first time they have heard that their violent past is anything but normal.

The last part of the Anger Recognition and Release class consists of taking the youth through the process of recognition and release. Again, as a number of youth cannot read or comprehend very well, I read aloud the following to the men and pause for discussion or questions. The prayer at the end is suggested and completely voluntary. Many times a youth has to steep in the recognition of the violence done to him before he is ready for release from his anger.

# ANGER RECOGNITION AND RELEASE

## Reason For This Class

The primary reason a Hope Now youth loses his job is when his anger gets out of control. Alcohol and drugs only make things worse. Out-of-control anger shows itself in your life in the following ways:

· Getting in a fight with your girlfriend/wife where you touch her in anger
· Getting in fights with her family or at parties

- Getting high or drunk
- Maddogging or fighting with a fellow worker
- Mouthing off to a boss
- Punching holes in walls or doors, or throwing things
- Cursing people or calling them names
- Doing things that wreck your future.

If the police are called in a domestic dispute, someone will be arrested for spousal abuse and almost every time it will be you. By the time you get out of jail, you will have lost your job. Unless we deal with the source of our anger, we will overreact when someone hurts us. Anger makes us not care about others or ourselves.

## Reasons For Your Anger

The greatest hurts creating the most anger happened when you were a child, because the situation was most out of your control. Although your parents did the best they knew how, sometimes their best was not good enough to keep you from being hurt. Some of the ways your parents may have hurt you are by:

- Not being there for you
- Being alcoholics and drug addicts
- Disciplining you using something besides their open hand
- Telling you that you are going to be a loser
- Calling you names
- Letting the streets raise you
- Wasting money on gambling, drugs, etc. so you stay hungry and poor
- Not listening to you
- Not caring for you.

Most youth join gangs looking for the caring, family life, and money they should have gotten at home. Some people deny that their parents didn't love them enough, because it hurts too much to believe that you were not loved or wanted by your parents. A bad relationship is seen as better than no relationship at all.

**Here is how God defines true love:** *"Love is patient and kind. Love is not jealous or boastful or proud or rude. Love is not angry, and it keeps no record of when it has been disrespected. It is never glad about unfairness but is happy whenever good wins out. Love never gives up, never loses faith in God, is always hopeful, and lasts through every tough time"* (I Corinthians 13:8-10). How does your childhood compare?

## What Does God Say About Anger?

*"Surely resentment destroys the fool..."* (Job 5:2). Resentment is anger held for a long time.

*"Stop your anger! Turn from your rage"* (Psalm 37:8).

*"Those who control their anger are smart; those with a quick temper will make mistakes"* (Proverbs 14:29).

*"Violent people deceive their own friends, leading them down a harmful path"* (Proverbs 16:29).

*"Don't sin by letting anger gain control over you. Don't let the sun go down while you're still angry"* (Ephesians 4:26).

Anger is the energy given by God to make something right which has gone wrong. What you do with your anger will determine who you are and what will happen to you.

## How Can God Help You Deal With Your Anger?

Concerning the Cross of Christ, the Bible says, *"It was our weaknesses he carried; it was our sorrows that weighed him down"* (Isaiah 53:4). A painful and lost childhood is a sorrow that we carry; and the anger (resentment) we have is both a weakness and a weapon we use to get our own way and keep others away. If you are tired of carrying the anger from your lost and painful childhood, Jesus can take it from you. Are you ready to let go of, to forgive the hurts of your childhood? If so, here's how:

1. Take time to write down all the hurtful events you can remember from your childhood. There is healing

even in writing these things down.

2.  Share these memories with your girlfriend/wife, not as excuses but as reasons for your behavior. There is healing in crying over your childhood.

3.  Place your anger on Christ's cross by praying a prayer like this:

> "Lord Jesus, I am tired of carrying the anger of my childhood which has made me sin against you and others. I lay down the weapon of my anger on your cross. Teach me to forgive others as you have forgiven me. Thank you for dying on the cross to forgive my anger and all my other sins. Help me to live as you want me to. In Jesus name. Amen."

The most successful use of this process has occurred when a youth goes home and follows steps 1 and 2 above, and then meets with a staff member to share the results of step 1. The youth is then invited to do step 3.

The remaining two classes, Job Support and Budgeting, are taught in a classroom setting by our Training Director. Job Support covers how to establish meaningful relationships at home that will support a youth holding a job. After meeting our basic physical needs, relationships are vital to meeting our need to belong, have self-esteem, and find purpose in life. God has created us for relationships with him and others. The most difficult relationship for most Hope Now youth is the one they have with a girlfriend or wife, who may also be the mother of their children. Having no role models of responsible manhood, these youth come to us heavily dependent on their girlfriends for sex, a place to live, transportation, money, and childcare. Many of them expect the girlfriend to be the mother they never had, and the girlfriend expects the guy to be the father she lacked. This clash of expectations leads to many fights and frequent spousal abuse, both of which provide abundant opportunities for missing work. Therefore, to help change a young man's lifestyle, we aim in this class to redefine what a man is, and what commitment and responsibility are.

To find out who we are, the class explores issues of trust,

one's own self-perception and the masks we wear. By examining the top five needs for a woman and the top five needs for a man, we aim to help a youth develop shared values with his girlfriend, to increase mutual respect leading to reciprocal trust. Some positive ways of looking at, and dealing with, conflict are provided and the importance of forgiveness is emphasized. Real men serve their families and reflect a loving heavenly Father to their children. It only takes a sperm to be a father, but it takes a lifetime of service and guidance to become a dad. True manhood is found in having a relationship with our heavenly Father, in being under and exhibiting loving authority.

Marriage, God's plan for a man and woman who love each other and want to bring security to their children, is rarely even considered if youth lack economic stability. It takes the wise expenditure of money for poor people to make a marriage work, so our Budgeting Class is an introduction to effective money management. Beginning with the youth's values and society's values concerning money and success, we draw contrasts with the Biblical view of money. The class asks youth to explore the costs of the goals they have, and how much time it may take to reach those goals. The use of credit cards is discussed and, frankly, discouraged, but Hope Now youth still may end up in thousands of dollars of credit card debt. Buying a newer vehicle, a young male goal, is likewise discouraged, but that doesn't stop a youth earning minimum wage from signing a loan for a $17,000 truck and adding $2000 wheels charged to his credit card.

After giving the Biblical warning that the borrower is a slave to the lender, we emphasize in the Budgeting Class that how much money you have is not as important as how you spend it. Finally, by preparing an actual budget of living expenses in our area, most students discover that they are not moving out on their own as quickly as they imagined. Orlando wisely summed up the choices a youth must continually make during training: "You either live with the pain of discipline or the pain of regret." We hope the pain of discipline will prepare each man for employment.

# CHAPTER 18

# Successful Job Placement

*In any society, it doesn't take long to see what the smart, capable people do to thrive. In the suburbs, with their better schools, safer places to live, and more-abundant job opportunities, smart kids apply themselves to education, athletics and legitimate jobs and businesses. Following this path often has more to do with being intelligent than with being morally good or bad. But the streets of Chicago and other cities constitute a completely different culture. There the really smart guys, the natural leaders, rise quickly to prominent positions in the gangs. Again, this isn't primarily a moral decision. But with gang leadership come the rewards of "success" - money, respect, power, and girls – the same things the suburban kids get from their more traditional pursuits.*

Gordon McLean
*Too Young To Die*

For Hope Now to penetrate the business community, it is important to make every effort to obtain entry-level job opportunities from one significant employer in the area. When Valley Children's Hospital hired our youth, we gained instant credibility with the business community. As you pray, speak and make contacts for Hope Now, always ask for jobs, and then doors will open. Don't wait narrowly focused on obtaining a "Christian" employer, because any community-minded, well-respected employer will do. Once you have that employer, be sure to gain permission to publicize that fact in every way you can, in your newsletter, on your stationary and when you speak. Follow-up by contacting your local Chamber of Commerce, manufacturer's associations and organization of human

relations professionals to seek their help in setting up meetings with light industrial and service employers.

Appropriate job development and suitable job placement
are crucial to the success of Hope Now For Youth. Referrals
for possible job openings come from a variety of sources. The
annual banquet provides several leads, as does speaking to various churches and organizations throughout the year. Current
employers recommend us to other businesses. Calling on current employers often reminds them of openings that Hope
Now youth could fill. There is sometimes a need for "cold
calling," which begins with sending a letter and a brochure to
the CEO of a potential employer of Hope Now youth. We
find that one cold contact out of three may ultimately develop into a job.

To give you an idea of the kind of employers who are employing Hope Now youth and the jobs being offered, here is a
list of those who were recognized as Community Plus Employers at our 2002 annual banquet, providing financial/in-
kind support as well as jobs.

- Denham Personnel Services – temporary jobs, some
  temp-to-hire jobs
- Radisson Hotel and Conference Center – housekeep-
  ing, maintenance
- City of Fresno – alley and street cleanup, weed abate-
  ment
- Derrel's Mini Storage – constructing storage lockers
- Di-Pro Inc. – manufacturing air brake actuators
- Bill Marvin Electric – electrical contracting
- Dunavant of California – seasonal cotton bale sample
  sorting, computing
- Kaiser Permanente Medical Center– sterile process-
  ing, records, janitorial
- The Presort Center – direct mailing
- City of Sanger – street repairing
- First Presbyterian Church – custodial
- Hye Quality Bakery – bakery assistant, shipping and
  receiving

- Irwin-Jackson & Co. – receptionist, bookkeeping (for wives/girlfriends)
- Orange Avenue Landfill – recycling
- CSE Homes – construction
- Fresno Meat Company – meat processing
- Fresno Plumbing & Heating – plumbing
- Paul Evert's RV Country – detailing and servicing recreational vehicles
- Saint Agnes Medical Center – housekeeping
- The Peoples Church – custodial
- Traveler's Body and Fender – auto body painting
- Vineyard Pools – pool construction, piping, landscaping

After the usual probationary period of employment, most of the above jobs include benefits available to the youth and his family.

Once a new employer has responded positively to our letter or a follow-up phone call, Executive Associate John Raymond or Job Developer Marty Minasian strives to make an appointment with the CEO and the direct supervisor to explain Hope Now. At that meeting, the following information is given to the prospective employer.

## HOW DOES AN EMPLOYER WORK WITH HOPE NOW FOR YOUTH?

1. The business must decide that it wants to be community-minded by reducing crime and violence through hiring at-risk young men prepared, screened and recommended by Hope Now. The young men that Hope Now works with may have criminal or driving records that are not yet cleared. Many must rely upon the bus or a bicycle for transportation to and from work.

2. After determining which entry-level or training positions are to be made available only to at-risk youth trained by Hope Now, the employer should communicate the job order,

requirements, and benefits to Hope Now, trusting Hope Now to screen and properly prepare the young man for the job. The employer should be certain that the young man's immediate supervisor embraces the idea of hiring an at-risk youth. Hope Now will present its ministry at the supervisory level at the convenience of the employer.

3. Hope Now will choose and present one young man for each position. As these youth have already experienced a lifetime of rejection, Hope Now will not present more than one youth for any position. For the same reason, we ask the employer not to open this position to other applicants.

4. Barring any major surprise discovered during the interview, the employer will hire the youth at the terms previously discussed with Hope Now.

5. Hope Now will continue to help the young man navigate life's problems, including family issues and court requirements, so that he can always give his best attention to being a productive employee.

6. Hope Now is always available to the employer to assist with any problems that might arise, and would like to occasionally visit the employee at his worksite. Our experience indicates that our youth become extremely loyal employees because they soon realize the magnitude of the opportunity they have been given.

7. If additional positions become available for at-risk youth, the employer is warned that it is best not to rely solely on a recommendation by one of our previously placed youth, as the suggested individual may not have been screened and prepared by Hope Now. To maintain quality control, it is best to request a placement directly from Hope Now. Working together with the employer, we want to do whatever we can to enable the young man to become a successful employee.

Many employers have tried to hire at-risk youth, only to have their goodwill incinerated by poor job performance, fraudulent worker's compensation claims or worse. Early on businesses need to be assured that the entry-level youth we provide usually will be more reliable, because Hope Now offers continuing support to help solve problems that may interfere with work performance. It is important that all supervisors of this youth understand that they are a vital link not only to making a good employee but also to turning a life around. Situations in which the CEO endorses the vision, but the youth's direct supervisor does not, are ripe for failure. Unfortunately, a few foremen have made racist comments, while some others never let the youth forget he was a former gang member. Both of these actions are destructive and demeaning. Astoundingly, on one occasion, a CEO even asked a Hope Now youth to buy drugs for him! In situations like these, in which resolution does not seem possible, we remove the youth from the company and place him elsewhere.

Other considerations in job placement include evaluating the visibility of a young man's tattoos in light of how much of the public he will be meeting. For a minor youth who can only work in a fast food restaurant, the need to have him employed near home is sometimes offset by the need to not have him visible to rival gang members from his neighborhood. Phillip came to Hope Now after graduation from the Elkhorn Correctional Facility, our juvenile boot camp. One night, after six months of successful work at McDonald's, he walked out back of the restaurant during a break only to be attacked by rival gang members. Phillip so strongly resisted the urge to fight back that, when the police came, they praised him for not escalating the confrontation. Choosing to err on the side of caution, we pulled Phillip from that job and placed him in a position at California State University Fresno where he was visible only to college students.

New employers are made aware that most of our youth are high school dropouts with criminal records, so for the business to require both a high school diploma and no criminal record sets up often insurmountable barriers to our youth's employment. To require a diploma or G.E.D. with no criminal record of violence for any employee is a standard some Hope Now youth can meet. No criminal record of drug possession or sales for a hospital employee can also be met. For an electronics warehouse to require no criminal record of theft is also understandable and achievable. Most jobs we seek, however, require only that a youth pass a drug test and be willing to work. A few jobs may require a driver's license and clean driving record, for forklift or auto work, which usually can be met if we are able to help a youth get his license.

Matching the right Hope Now youth with the job and meeting the specific needs of the employer are both central to proper placement. The Executive Associate ascertains the details of the job including work hours, pay and pay periods, benefits and any special requirements. He then explains that we will choose the best man we have available at the time for the job and will bring him for the interview. Making the right match includes determining if a youth wants to do the specific work, can work the particular shift, and is able to get himself to the job. We ask the employer to trust our ability to choose and not to ask us to bring more than one man for one job. We also ask that the employer not interview others for this position, because we want the Hope Now youth to experience the success of getting a job, not the rejection of being passed over. These youth have enough rejection in their lives without us setting them up for more. In summary, then, the employer must want to hire a Hope Now youth for this position.

The Executive Associate explains that, with the employer, we will form a triangle of success for this youth. If the young man shows up late or misses a day, we ask to be informed so that we can work alongside the employer to effect good job performance. Sometimes it takes a paycheck or two for a gang youth to begin to experience the power of "clean" money. If we are notified of transportation problems, the gift of a used men's bicycle sometimes does the trick. Hope Now is always available to help employer and employee develop a good working relationship that results in excellent job performance.

The employer packet includes the following information delineating the commitment we make and the commitment we seek.

## TWO ESSENTIAL COMMITMENTS
## MADE BY HOPE NOW AND THE EMPLOYER

### Our Commitment to the Employer

1. We will screen and recommend a young man for employment.

2. We will provide the young man with basic training relating to appearance and attitude.

3. We will maintain a caring and helping relationship with the at-risk youth during the term of his employment so as to minimize any risk of failure.

4. We will remain accessible to the employer to assist in any way requested to make our referral as productive an employee as possible.

5. We will be available to provide additional referrals for employment.

### The Employer's Commitment to the Employee

1. The young man will be treated with acceptance and respect, as would any employee of your company.

2. The employer will pay the young man a fair wage, giving raises as earned.

3. Recognizing the troubled background of the young man, the employer may choose to assist with special training in areas of timeliness, the handling of his money, etc.

4. The employer will allow occasional visits by the Vocational Placement Counselor or other Hope Now staff to check on the progress of the young man. The staff member will check in at the office prior to visiting the employee.

5. The employer will notify Hope Now for Youth if the work or attitude of the employee is unsatisfactory, recognizing our willingness to assist with the problem, if requested.

Clearly delineated expectations of Hope Now, the employer

and the employee are key to the successful placement of any youth.

Once the job offer has been received, if time allows, the best candidates are determined at the weekly staff meeting. The Executive Associate usually discusses position openings requiring immediate placement with the Executive Director, Training Director or the counselor. Several possible candidates are normally selected and prioritized, as it may be impossible to contact a youth in time or a youth may have a reason why he can't take a particular job. A youth's ability to get to a job with reliable transportation is an important consideration to be discussed. Relying on a friend or a girlfriend is not considered a reliable choice, while a parent might prove dependable. Using public transportation, a bicycle or a car appears to be the best option.

The Executive Associate needs to be kept abreast of all youth who are ready for jobs, whether first-timers or old-timers. Upon the completion of training, as certified by the counselor, the Training Director does a Preplacement Interview. If a first-time youth demonstrates that he has learned what he needs to know to succeed and has the proper identification for work, the Executive Associate will then interview him. If the position being offered is a starter job, at minimum wage and without benefits, it almost always goes to a first-timer. If the opening is at a higher wage and has benefits, it may be offered to any youth who is available and whom we believe to be qualified.

The candidate is told ahead of time to dress in the best clothes he has that are appropriate to the job, to be well groomed, and to remove any face or tongue jewelry and earrings. The Executive Associate picks him up and takes him to the interview. During the initial telephone contact and the ride to the interview, the youth is asked about the last time he took drugs, because almost all employers administer drug tests. If a youth tells us he's clean and fails the drug test, thereby threatening future placements with a company, he is almost always dropped from the program. If we approve his reentry into Hope Now at a later time, he must pay for and pass a drug test. The following information is discussed both in the telephone contact and during the ride to the interview.

## HOW TO INTERVIEW FOR A JOB

1.  Look your best!
    A. Clean clothes
    B. Clean shave
    C. Hair neat and combed
    D. No earrings, no face/tongue jewelry
    E. Regular shoes - no sandals
    F. Nice shirt and pants

2.  Have a good attitude!
    A. Speak clearly and loud enough to be heard. Don't worry about your language skills - do your best.
    B. Smile
    C. Be yourself. You don't want them to hire someone you are pretending to be.

3.  Be prepared!
    A. Take two forms of identification: Social Security card and driver's license or other picture identification.
    B. Be ready to ask a question about the company. Ask your counselor in advance if you need help with ideas. Sample: "What opportunities are there for advancement in this company?"
    C. Have in your mind what position you are applying for. Ask your counselor in advance if you are unsure. Don't say: "I can do anything" or "I'll take whatever is available"
    Better to say: "I am willing to learn how to assemble sprinklers."
    D. Bring your practice application with the addresses and phone numbers of references and of previous employers, if you had any.

E. Employers sometimes ask, "Tell me about yourself' or "What would you like to be doing five years from now?" Have a brief answer ready.

4. Be Truthful!
   A. Truthfully saying you have no previous employment is better than lying about it.
   B. Be honest about drugs. They will probably test you and find out anyway, and tests don't make mistakes.
   C. If the application asks about conviction for a felony, be honest. Never mislead an employer.
   D. Take responsibility for your past - Avoid phrases like "they didn't..." or "the job was boring." It is better to say, "I'm changing and learning. I'm ready to do a good job here."

The Executive Associate may or may not sit in on the interview, as desired by the employer. Barring any major faux pas, the youth is told that he has the job, pending his passing the drug test. The smile the Executive Associate sees at that announcement is abundant reward for all the effort. This young man is on his way into the American mainstream because God and the "whole village" worked together to help him.

# CHAPTER 19

# Partnering with the Sectors

*Violence is not something you stop by preaching. Violence disappears as children experience success and discipline and begin believing in their own possibilities. While they were members of El Santo Nino, they got back on the track to growing up – they became part of a village with concerned adults preparing children to take a proper place among them. Those students who managed to find this again after the gang school at El Santa Nino closed are alive, sober and enjoying this day. For those who did not, growing up stopped and they went back to wandering the periphery of this village, struggling for a way back in.*

Arturo Hernandez
*Peace in the Streets*

Getting the Church, government, and private business to partner together in tackling city crime and violence was apparently a unique and sometimes unsettling idea. Early on we tried to find Christian businessmen to hire our youth, even contacting a group of Christian businessmen. Meeting with no success, however, we turned elsewhere. The idea that nonbelieving business owners could accomplish the will of God was shocking to churches and Christian community-based organizations alike. City government, for its part, couldn't even conceive of assisting an overtly Christian organization to accomplish even secular civic functions, like crime reduction and full employment. Private business was the least scandalized by the approach of Hope Now, because all they wanted were good employees. But even here, our concept of reciprocity, "if you're profiting from this city, you need to help improve it," took some selling. Hope Now's message to each of the sectors was, "If we only do what we have always done, we will only get what we've already got."

Our message to Christians was to think out of the box, to expand their view of how God gets things done. Since God could enable even a jackass to see an angel and speak, (Numbers 22:21-31) he could use anybody, believer or unbeliever alike, to accomplish his purposes. Both secular government and secular business could bless the lives of gang youth with dignity and productivity. Hope Now, therefore, appealed to all people of goodwill and offered them an opportunity in the midst of a crime calamity to make a difference. As Sir Winston Churchill remarked, "A pessimist sees the difficulty in every opportunity; an optimist sees the opportunity in every difficulty." Fresno, as is true of your city today, had many optimists ready to seize the opportunity.

In speaking to business owners and managers, Hope Now emphasized the costs of crime and violence, not only in taxes, but also in quality of life. The effect of graffiti on their neighborhoods was blight, reducing their property values. Vandalism and theft were additional costs. Their ability to attract professional-level employees was hampered by being located in a city known as the car theft capital of California. Perhaps the most compelling argument for many employers was the opportunity they had, with Hope Now's help, to change a young person's life with a job. They know young people can change – many of today's employers did when they were younger, with someone's help. Our message was clear: "The power to change the direction of at-risk youth is in the hands of the corporations and businesses of our city."

One other offer Hope Now made that was attractive to businesses was providing *reliable* entry-level workers. A business that had turned us down because our youth lacked welding experience called recently and said, "Please send us somebody who can pass a drug test and show up at work. Right now we are training our janitor to weld." This employer had interviewed five people who applied through newspaper advertising and decided that three of them had enough welding experience to qualify for a position. But all three flunked the drug test! Darlene Gadley of the Youth Employment Service has said, "Without a support structure, ninety percent of these youth will crash and burn." Hope Now workers are more reliable because we are their support structure, helping them successfully navigate life's problems so that they can focus on staying employed.

Obtaining the help of city government was not even contemplated at the beginning, but it should have been. Our first Development Director Kaye Cummings broke the ice by speaking with Mayor Jim Patterson in 1996 at a reception for the Boys & Girls Clubs, challenging him to provide both jobs and funds. Her rationale was simple: "Even though we are an evangelical Christian organization, Hope Now performs a necessary secular civic function by reducing gang crime, graffiti and violence through job training and placement. Let the city financially support the civic functions Hope Now offers and, as a major employer, supply jobs for our trained youth." Fresno has done precisely that since 1997.

The City and County of Fresno have been blessed with outspoken Christian leaders in government, including our Mayor, Police Chief and County Sheriff. However, Hope Now has still been the victim of apparently anti-Christian bias before one board and one committee that make recommendations on funding. A county board asked me how we could separate the religious portion of our ministry from the job training and placement portion. I replied that while the Christian values of honesty, thrift, and hard work are certainly part of our job training, we believe that getting youth away from committing crimes and violence was certainly a secular civic function worthy of county support. It wasn't. A city committee asked only one question of us, "Do you provide services to gays, lesbians, bisexuals and transgender individuals?" I replied that we don't raise that issue, but if it arises, we provide services regardless. Sexual preference is irrelevant to needing a job to get off the streets. Apparently that answer also wasn't good enough to keep our city funding from being slashed more than any other organization. Nevertheless, holding to a clearly defined vision, we take our lumps and continue striving to do excellently what God has called us to do. One thing we do not take is any money that restricts our ministry or the scope of our work. We will not choose to be politically correct at the expense of becoming spiritually impotent.

Keeping your focus is essential as you partner with the various sectors. A church may want you to form a youth group of gang kids, which really is the Church's job, not yours. City government may want you to work with young women as well, who certainly need help but have a different set of problems to overcome. Businesses may want to put Hope Now youth through several weeks of full-time unpaid training before they will hire them. That's all well and good, but gang youth will still be running the streets all night, stealing stereos and selling drugs to survive. Those activities mean they will not show up daily for training. That unpaid training is not solving their economic problem, so their chances of successful completion are nil.

When you do partner with the other sectors, make sure the goal will benefit the gang youth with whom you work. Before Hope Now entered the City of Fresno competition for nonprofit organizations that would participate in the All-America City contest, we decided that Fresno becoming an All-America City would improve the quality of life for all of us, gain Hope Now greater recognition for funding, and provide more jobs for Hope Now youth. That coveted 2000 All-America City designation has changed how Fresno thinks about itself and did improve our funding from the community. The city's growing self-confidence has also helped the community keep a Triple A baseball team by building a downtown stadium where, hopefully, some future Hope Now youth will be employed. In 2001, Hope Now again responded to the invitation of the City by writing a letter of support for obtaining an Empowerment Zone designation from the federal government. Fresno was one of only ten cities chosen for the award, which offers tax advantages for businesses to locate in some of the poorest parts of our city. The positive results for our youth from poverty areas, we believed, would be self-evident.

Although our direct contact with police officers or deputy sheriffs is minimal, we do need contact with probation and parole officers. For that purpose we have developed the following legal release form.

## HOPE NOW FOR YOUTH AND THE FRESNO COUNTY PROBATION DEPARTMENT RELEASE OF INFORMATION

I hereby authorize the Fresno County Probation Department to release information regarding my background, offense history, and probation performance to Hope Now For Youth. This information will be used to develop and implement a plan for my treatment and rehabilitation. I also authorize Hope Now For Youth to release information regarding my attendance, performance and progress to the Fresno County Probation Department.

This Release of Information will remain in force until I submit a written authorization requesting cancellation to both Hope Now For Youth and the Fresno County Probation Department.

My Probation Officer's name is: _____

My Probation Officer's telephone is: _____

Your Signature: _____

Print Your Name: _____

My Birth Date is: _____

Today's Date is: _____

My Age at Time of Offense: _____

Witnessed by: _____

Print Name: _____

Date: _____

A similar release is provided for parole agents of the California Department of Corrections and the California Youth Authority. When asking a youth to sign this release, we emphasize that Hope Now is not an extension of the probation or parole department. About the only time we use this release is when a youth has been jailed on a violation of probation or parole and we want to find out what has happened and how long he will be incarcerated. This enables us to notify his place of work, and to determine whether or not the employer can hold the young man's job for him. A staff member also will visit the youth in jail and ask him what happened. The Sheriff's Department has granted Hope Now staff jail passes for non-contact visits. If it is determined that a youth has been using Hope Now to con his probation officer, this release enables us to inform the officer that the youth has been dropped from our program.

Working with the Church, government, and private business sectors involves developing and maintaining strong relationships with the key players in each. By regularly taking part in Pastor's Prayer Summits, God led me to meet Pastor Rod Suess of Butler Avenue Mennonite Brethren Church, which became one of our supporting and base churches. Through accepting an invitation to join the Rotary Club of Fresno, I have gotten to know employers, civic leaders and donors who now back our work. When asked by a council member, I offer a prayer at the Fresno City Council meeting. To show gratitude for their actions supporting long-term improvements in our community, I make personal contributions to the campaigns of those city leaders who help Hope Now. Leadership Fresno is a one-year training program for civic leaders I completed in 1997. By means of these involvements, the work of Hope Now is exposed to leaders in the larger community, leaders whose support is so vital to our success.

When we started Hope Now For Youth, I thought that all we needed to do to change the life direction of a gang youth was to mobilize the sectors to encourage him and employ him. I discovered that we serve a merciful God who doesn't show us more of the vision than we can accept. Many more of these young men had sired children than I had expected, and therefore had to learn to be fathers and to relate to the mothers of their children. Early on, we decided that we could not change the home life of the families these young men were born into, but now God was revealing that we could affect the families that they were so desperately trying to form. With no role models or horrible role models, these young men knew what they didn't want to be but had no idea what they should be. Most of the young men's girlfriends or wives were just as dysfunctional, and for the same reasons. They all needed a lot more long-term caring and support than I could have ever imagined.

# CHAPTER 20

# The Extras of Caring

*For men, marriage is the precondition, the enabling context, for fatherhood as a social role. Why? Because marriage fosters paternal certainty, thus permitting emergence of what anthropologists call the legitimacy principle. This is my child, not another man's child. In turn paternal certainty permits and encourages paternal investment: the commitment of the father to the well-being of the child.*

David Blankenhorn
*Fatherless America*

When we see a feat of daring on television, the comment is often made, "Don't try this at home." As to what you're going to learn about in this chapter, I would say, "Don't try this at first." Only as you increase staff will you be able to do some of these things. Keep your eyes on the first priority goal: to get gang young men away from crime and violence and into a job. As you strive to eliminate any obstacle to his being a successful employee, each Hope Now youth will present you a series of problems to be solved. The primary need to make him a responsible father and husband will press in on you as you try to keep a particular young man working

If there is one crime that most often makes our youth lose their jobs, it is spousal abuse. Attending the Anger Recognition and Release Class and the Job Support Class on relationships is required of each Hope Now youth. On an occasional basis, furthermore, we offer Marriage and Family Classes where up to four couples can receive some modeling of and teaching in how to sustain a loving and affirming marriage relation-ship. We host these once a week sessions for four weeks at a home, where we can also share a meal together. If the couples cannot find childcare, a church location with childcare facili-ties may be an option. Another consideration is having trans-portation to and from the class.

The first session of the class covers what it means to be a Christian, which is the basis of a Christian marriage. Here we cover the three relationships of marriage: a personal relation-ship with Christ by each spouse in addition to the marriage relationship (Ephesians 5:21-33). Marriage is God's idea and only with his help can we work it out with joy. Topics for the remaining sessions include dealing with anger and offering forgiveness (Ephesians 4:25-32), handling money (Matthew 6:19-34), and maintaining sexual fidelity (I Corinthians 6:9-20).

The most difficult part of this class is getting the couples to attend all four sessions. To those who do, we give a copy of *Baby & Child Care* published by Focus on the Family (www.focusonthefamily.org). The night before each session, I make phone call reminders, but even then only half the couples finish the class. If you only find joy when they attend all ses-sions, you will be a very unhappy person. But if you believe that whatever they received, in however many sessions they attended, is more than they had before, you can still find joy. Remember, however, that this sporadic attendance can make it frustrating for whoever has to plan the meals.

At this class we once again remind them of who they re-ally are. These are the statements we have been making to the young man since he entered Hope Now, to counter his up-bringing and the negative influences of our society. It is good for him to hear them again and for his girlfriend to hear them for the first time.

## WHO ARE YOU?

Knowing who you are determines what kind of future you will have. What you believe about yourself affects what happens to you. Satan, through this sinful world, lies to you about who you are. Only God, through his Word (The Bible), tells you the truth.

· The Lie: <u>You are nothing but an animal that evolved from other animals.</u>

   **The Truth:** You were created by God to be like him - *"So God created man in his own image, in the image of God he created him; male and female he created them"* (Genesis 1:27).

· The Lie: <u>You are very small and insignificant in this vast universe.</u>

   **The Truth:** You are of great value and known by God - *"And even the very hairs of your head are all numbered. So don't be afraid; you are worth more than many sparrows"* (Matthew 10:30).

· The Lie: <u>When you die, it's all over, so grab all you can now.</u>

   **The Truth:** You have an eternal soul that will live beyond physical death - *"All those who sleep in the dust of the earth will awake: some to everlasting life, others to shame and everlasting destruction"* (Daniel 12:2).

· The Lie: <u>The way to happiness is getting sex, money, drugs, drink, things and power.</u>

   **The Truth:** The greatest joy is doing what you were made for, to know and serve God - *"You have given me greater joy than those who have rich harvests of grain and wine"* (Psalm 4:7).

· The Lie: <u>You'll always be a failure, like those around you, so why try?</u>

   **The Truth:** God working in you changes everything - *"Jesus replied, 'What is impossible with men is possible with God'"* (Luke 18:27).

· The Lie: <u>Nobody and nothing comes before loyalty to your family.</u>

**The Truth:** A relationship with God and obedience to his commandments come before loyalty to your family - *"Don't think that I have come to bring peace to the earth! No, I came to bring a sword. I have come to set a man against his father, and a daughter against her mother, and a daughter-in-law against her mother-in-law. Your enemies will be right in your own household! If you love your father or mother more than you love me, you are not worthy of being mine; or if you love your son or daughter more than me, you are not worthy of being mine. If you refuse to take up your cross and follow me, you are not worthy of being mine. If you cling to your life, you will lose it; but if you give it up for me, you will find it"* (Matthew 10:34-39).

· **The Lie:** <u>There are many ways to relate to God and obey him</u>.

**The Truth:** Since there is only one God, there is only one Way in which we can relate and obey - *"Jesus answered, 'I am the way and the truth and the life. No one comes to the Father except through me...Anyone who has seen me has seen the Father...The words you hear are not my own; they belong to the Father who sent me.'"* (John 14:6,9,24).

As most of the couples in these classes are not married, we emphasize that marriage is God's plan for families and the greatest protection for their children. They don't want their children to experience the abandonment many of them experienced, yet sexual sin and the hyper-individualism promoted by our society battle against God's plan. So we turn once again to God's Word for guidance.

## WHAT IS YOUR RELATIONSHIP?

God wants to bring you joy in marriage. Satan, through this sinful world, encourages sex as soon and as often as possible with as many people as possible. The unshown and unspoken result is babies, many of whom will grow up without the nurture and guidance of a father. Satan wants it that way because the biggest doorway to God the Father is having a loving father. If he can shut that door, he will shut out many people from knowing God. Satan lies to you about marriage and family, but God, through his Word (the Bible), tells the truth.

· The Lie: <u>Sex is just another appetite, like hunger, to be satisfied whenever and with whomever you want.</u>

**The Truth:** Sexual sin (intercourse outside of marriage) lessens your ability to bond in marriage and have a stable family - *"You may say, 'I am allowed to do anything.' But I reply, 'Not everything is good for you.' And even though 'I am allowed to do anything,' I must not become a slave to anything. 'Food is for the stomach and the stomach is for food.' This is true, though someday God will destroy both of them. Our bodies were not meant for sexual immorality, but for the Lord, and the Lord for the body... Run away from sexual sin! No other sin affects the body like this one. Sexual immorality is a sin against your own body"* (I Corinthians 6:12,13,18).

· The Lie: <u>The purpose of getting married is to make me happy.</u>

**The Truth**: God says your purpose is to make your spouse happy — *"A newly married man must not be drafted into the army or given any other special responsibilities. He must be free to be at home for one year, bringing happiness to the wife he has married"* (Deuteronomy 24:5).

· The Lie: <u>If things don't work out we can break up or get a "no-fault" divorce.</u>

**The Truth**: Divorce is not an option in marriage - *"A man leaves father and mother and is joined to his wife, and the two unite into one. Since they are no longer two but one, let no one separate them, for God has joined them together...A man who divorces his wife and marries another commits adultery—unless his wife has been unfaithful...A wife must not separate from her husband. But if she does leave him, let her remain single or else go back to him and the husband must not separate from his wife..."* (Matthew 19:5,6,9; I Corinthians 7:10,11).

· The Lie: <u>Divorce or separation is nobody's business but ours. Abortion is a woman's right.</u>

**The Truth**: Divorce is God's business and your children's business - *"Don't you know that your body is the temple of the Holy Spirit, who lives in you and was given to you by God? You do not belong to yourself, for God bought you with a high price. So you must honor God with your body... Didn't the Lord make you one with your wife? In body and spirit you are his. And what does he want? Godly children from your union. So guard yourself; remain loyal to the wife of your youth. 'For I hate divorce!' says the Lord, the God of Israel...So guard yourself; always remain loyal to your wife'"* (I Corinthians 6:19,20; Malachi 2:15,16).

· The Lie: <u>Living together is OK, because marriage is just a piece of paper.</u>

**The Truth**: God says that the sexually immoral are going to hell- *"Don't you know that those who do wrong will have no share in the Kingdom of Heaven? Don't fool yourselves. Those who indulge in sexual sin, who are idol worshippers, adulterers, prostitutes, homosexuals, thieves, greedy people, drunkards, abusers, swindlers — none of these will have a share in the Kingdom of Heaven... But cowards who turn away from me, and unbelievers, and the corrupt, and murderers, and the sexually immoral, and those who practice witchcraft, and idol worshippers, and all liars — their doom is in the lake that burns with fire and sulfur. This is the second death"* (I Corinthians 6:9,10; Revelation 21:8).

· The Lie: <u>God cannot forgive sexual sin; it is the unforgivable sin.</u>

**The Truth**: The only unforgivable sin is to not accept Christ's forgiveness — *"Those who indulge in sexual sin...adulterers...prostitutes...homosexuals... There was a time when some of you were just like that, but now your sins have been washed away, and you have been set apart for God. You have been made right because of what the Lord Jesus Christ and* *the Spirit of our God have done for you... If wicked people turn away from all their sins and begin to obey my laws and do what is just and right, they will surely live and not die. All their past sins will be forgotten..."* (I Corinthians 6:9-11; Ezekiel 18:21).

The second session of our Marriage and Family Class was to begin at 6:30 pm with dinner that my wife had made. I had reminded the couples the night before, as it is hard for them to keep schedules in unscheduled lives. By 6:45 pm no one had come. I called all the couples again and got one answering machine, followed by a youth who told me what he thought I wanted to hear and but then actually didn't come. Finally, I reached Josh. He said they would come in half an hour. Marilyn and I ate, not knowing for sure if anyone would come. At 7:15 pm Josh and Teresa came.

The evening's topic was to be a discussion of Christian love, including how to praise and criticize. But before I could get to the topic, Josh said one word, "forgiveness." Neither Josh nor Teresa could forgive the other for the past, even though they had recently given their lives to Jesus and had received his forgiveness. So I told the story of the ungrateful servant from Matthew 18:21-35, who was forgiven by the king but still couldn't forgive his fellow servant. Josh and Teresa listened to the story but proceeded to keep arguing round and round. Then I asked about the parents they grew up with. Josh's parents were drug addicts who always betrayed him. His mother valued her drugs above him. Teresa's father abandoned her and her stepfather blamed her when he divorced her mother. The men in her life were not to be trusted. Josh needed Teresa to cherish him and Teresa needed Josh to be trustworthy. As so often happens, they were bringing childhood needs to adult relationships. I gave them the right to say, whenever feelings of worthlessness or suspicion arose, "I am not your parent." They left arm-in-arm, laughing at the saying, and planning to attend our Pismo Beach campout. I knew, however, that there was still a long and difficult road up ahead of them.

Another occasional class we offer is Christian Parenting, taught by Executive Associate John Raymond and his wife Edith. This four-week seminar teaches parents the Biblical plan for child rearing. It deals with discipline methods, teaching behavior by example, and how to communicate effectively with children. By encouraging positive affirmation and praise in parenting, this seminar reduces the possibility of responding to disobedience with child abuse. If parents have not already received a copy of the book, *Baby & Child Care*, one is given to them during the class. In addition to offering these classes, John and Edith often travel to a youth's home to offer personalized marriage and family counseling.

Family campouts, beach trips or a day of fishing add a further dimension of caring, giving the staff an opportunity to observe youth families in action. Training Director Bob Pankratz, working with the street staff, organizes this deeper level of caring to youth who are already working and their families. Hearts are unburdened to an amazing degree as youth sit around a campfire at night. The experience of hiking a mountain or swimming in a rock pool or being flattened by a wave broadens the horizons of those whose view has been blunted by the city. They begin to understand that there is a great and powerful God who is big enough to care for them. Every tree points to its maker and each bird and brook sings his praise.

I believe that Christ also laughs and has a good time on these trips. When we took 15 youth to Avila Beach, Boun and Sou played checkers, which doesn't sound special unless we remember that a few years ago Boun shot at Sou. At the next campsite was a woman who, seeing all these gang kids, said to her family, "There goes our camping weekend!" By the next day, however, after our men were in Bible Study and well behaved, she had the courage to admit what she had said, "Please forgive me. I'm a new Christian and judged you guys wrongly." She had witnessed a miracle of Jesus.

One extension of caring which was not successful was an attempt to provide some level of residential living by partially underwriting the rent of an apartment. The Hope Now Living Unit was located on the property of a home owned by a Christian couple that has chosen to live in the inner city. Omar's failure triggered this idea. A single man with a prison record who grew up watching his mother engage in prostitution, Omar worked successfully for over a year and had given his heart to the Lord. But he was living in an apartment building populated with drug dealers and pimps. Low wages and poor budgeting usually mandate poverty level workers living in substandard housing. All too predictably, Omar got picked up on a parole violation for being with negative associates, and went off for another year in prison. For the few youth who are desperate like Omar, and homeless, the Hope Now Christian Living Unit appeared to be an answer. But all the youth we placed there over a two-year period failed on their jobs. One returned to prison and another graffitied the closet and dresser. For those on the edge, even this assistance did not offer enough caring.

Some people have asked why we don't include community service as a regular part of our training program. Occasionally, we have gone on canoe trips that we earn by helping clean up the San Joaquin River. As we paddle along, we soak each other. Twice we have enjoyed snow camps where the youth planted hundreds of seedlings in Sequoia National Forest. These experiences are certainly new ones for our youth and they enjoy them; we even count the work as an odd job, although no one gets paid. This limitation presents the first problem with community service: a gang youth needs to receive money for his work so he can survive, or else he will still sell drugs and steal to eat. Next, to be able to "give back" to the community, you first have to believe that the community has given something to you. Gang youth aren't there yet. Finally, since our courts use community service as a punishment for crime, it may take years before volunteering becomes a joyful obligation.

Four times a year we hold Hope Now Family gatherings. At the Annual Banquet in February, youth who are receiving successful work awards and others brought by their employers enjoy an evening like they have never known. Eating out has always been fast food and never with so many people. During the summer we offer a three-on-three basketball tournament and family barbeque with a bounce house, the format originally being developed by Training Director Bob Pankratz working with two summer interns. Our God cares that youth enjoy living and find time to play. Bob also helps us celebrate Thanksgiving and Christmas with family dinners that can include free turkeys, coupons for Christmas trees, Christmas crafts and toys for the children. The most special gifts for the adults are the hand-made quilts donated by the talented and caring women of Easterby-Knox Presbyterian Church. At our first Thanksgiving Dinner in 1997 we hosted 27 young men and 17 wives/girlfriends discussing how to better communicate, to encourage, to manage anger, and to forgive. Nothing is unusual here, until you realize that the laughter and excitement are being generated by ex-gang members with criminal records, including assault with a deadly weapon, robbery, burglary, attempted murder, grand theft auto, and carjacking. Most have been imprisoned, some up to one-third of their short lives, because they couldn't control their rage until they experienced the love of Jesus. Attending each of these holiday dinners are those who will hear for the first time the true reasons for the season. The caring God is further revealed through the gift of his Son to our world, and we are thankful.

At special events like the dinners and through our placed youth, we meet the family of many young men. Once a young man has successfully held a job for several months, if his girlfriend, wife or sister wants a job, we try to place them, often through Denham Personnel Services. Though we offer no special training to young women, many of them succeed. Most have had more education and work experience than the Hope Now youth.

Through the dedication of our first Development Director, Kaye Bonner Cummings, a Hope Now Scholarship Fund was established at the State Center Community College District for youth who want to attend our local community colleges. Each semester we have from three to ten Hope Now scholars, former gang youth who are moving ahead with their undergraduate education. Benny was one of the first. When his best friend was killed in a drive-by shooting, Benny began reexamining his gang involvement and decided he needed to do something to get out. "That's when I met up with Hope Now For Youth," he says. "They got me a few odd jobs to see if I was serious, and then put me in a permanent job. They supported all my decisions. 'You want to go to school?' and before I know it, I'm getting scholarships to go to college." Benny even made the Dean's List for academic achievement at Fresno City College. When he got all A's in his first semester, he pointed to his head and said, "There really is something up there!" What a spectacular discovery for a gang youth!

The extras of caring may be provided by the Vocational Placement Counselor or other staff as they help a youth with any of the services we offer.

## SERVICES PROVIDED BY STAFF

**Life Skills and Job Preparation**
-Recruitment and Intake
-Relationship Building
-Parenting and Mentoring
-Christian Values Formation and Training
-Work Ethic Training
-Vocational Counseling
-Job Development
-Job Placement
-On-the-job Visits
-Legal Assistance – donated
-Medical and Dental Assistance – donated
-Psychological Counseling - partially donated
-Obtaining Identification
-Obtaining Driver's Licenses
-Tattoo Removal – when available through Fresno County
-Drug Testing and Drug and Alcohol Rehabilitation Referral

-Recreational Activities and Trips
-Follow-up and Relationship Maintenance

**Classes**
-Job Success, Job Search, Job Support, Budgeting,
     Anger Recognition and Release, Addictions Awareness
-Tax Filing
-Bible Study (optional)
-Discipling and Spiritual Development (optional)

**Further Education**
-Encouraging Return to School
-Hope Now Scholarship Fund (State Center
     Community College District)

**Services for Women and Families**
-Family Dinners, Values Lectures, Group Discussion
-Women's Job Development and Placement
-Marriage and Family Classes and Counseling
-Parenting Classes
-Campouts, Picnics, Conferences

Every bit of caring helps a youth better care for himself. Ironically, once I got into a heated e-mail exchange with a foundation that stated it wanted to "expand access to affordable, quality health care for underserved individuals and communities." Try as I might I could not convince the program officer that poor gang members working at jobs with health benefits accomplished what the foundation wanted. That exchange reminded me again of how unique Hope Now is in promoting self-sufficiency. It apparently is a revolutionary idea that poor gang members do not have to further depend on agency largesse, supported by foundations, but can work to obtain their own health care. Blessed are those youth who have been touched by any part of this revolution.

# CHAPTER 21

# They Always Leave Better

*The true measure of a man is how he treats someone who can do him absolutely no good.*
Samuel Johnson (1709-1784)

Isaac saw him in the Department of Motor Vehicles line and yelled out, "John Raymond!" Isaac would not have been one of those youth we had considered a success, even though he worked a little over two months. He quit his job abruptly, losing any hope of benefits, because he thought he had cancer. A few days later we dropped him when we found out that he had encouraged another Hope Now youth to go to Mexico to buy drugs. But then here he was, calling out to our Executive Associate, and so mainstreamed looking that he was unrecognizable. Isaac assured John that he was doing all right now and had been working steadily for over a year and a half. The caring invested into Isaac had paid off. But the youth whom Isaac had encouraged to buy drugs, after getting married and buying a home, had lost his four-year job with benefits because of alcohol and drug addiction. Refusing to get help, that youth went from wheeling a pushcart, to working fast food, to being unemployed. Two beautiful children are being ignored for drugs, just like he and his wife had been when they were young.

If you are going to get involved in the lives of gang members, prepare for both heartbreak and happiness. You'll get discouraged when, after holding a job for almost three years, a youth goes back to his full-blown drug addiction on the streets.

Previously he had refused to attend or had bombed out of any rehabilitation program suggested by the staff. At this point he leaves a wife and two beautiful children behind. You'll fear for their safety, and with good reason. In one week, a bullet went all the way through Tyrone's home, two of Dua's passengers were wounded in a drive-along shooting, and five shots punched through the chair Kou normally sits on to play computer games. You'll definitely lose some of the young men you'll meet. Several of our youth have been killed, one in a robbery he was committing. Two committed suicide: one overdosed on drugs and the other shot himself and a girlfriend when surrounded by police after a robbery. Another young man died in a drunken stupor. Our hearts break while we pray for the families and for each other.

There is a special urgency to gang intervention. Pedro had been through our training program and was waiting for a job. Although we emphasized the need for patience, Pedro said that he was discouraged because he wasn't getting a job, so decided to get "drunk and stupid." Pedro was arrested for disorderly conduct and discharging a firearm. Because this was his second strike, he's facing six years in prison. Tragically, on the same day he was jailed, we had a job available for Pedro. If only he had waited, or the job had been offered sooner, the outcome would have been different.

Get ready too for the iceberg phenomenon – you're only going to see one-ninth of the good you are doing. Roy came back recently, still smelling of the five months he had just spent in jail for missing his probation appointments. Once you have been inside a penal institution, even to visit, you'll never forget the odor of sweaty bodies and unwashed souls. Stress, anger and fear have a stench all their own. His mom was in jail for drugs; his father was a drunkard who didn't work. No wonder Roy said, "Hope Now was the best thing that ever happened to me." He lost a good job a year earlier for being late too many times, but now he says he is serious because he has a baby to support. Besides, Roy doesn't want his younger brother to follow him and end up in prison. Considering all the bad influences he has in his life, we said that only if he gets serious about Jesus and hanging out with Jesus' people does he stand a chance. We are praying for Roy.

I just got a call from Lee. He left his name at a booth we were manning at a church missions fair. We were asking for church people to give us odd jobs or regular jobs for our youth. Lee was just looking for a job. God brought us together. Lee was living with his father in Santa Ana, but his father was taken to jail. He can't live here with his mother because she attacks him. With all these life problems, it's no wonder this 17-year-old has dropped out of school just three months short of graduation. He said he never really joined a gang because he didn't want to waste his time or lose his life defending turf he doesn't own. If he does what is right and finds a job, some friends will let Lee stay with them. After applying at 20 different places, Lee was pretty discouraged. How could you *not* help someone like Lee? Anything you do *for* him is better than what has been done *to* him. After explaining the program, I gave him the pager of one of our counselors. Lee sounds like a young man who wants to help himself, but you never know. What I do know is that we will be available to help him if he takes the initiative to call.

A study of employment patterns in an impoverished Brooklyn, New York neighborhood suggests that the primary reason for ghetto unemployment is not the lack of nearby jobs but the absence of social networks that provide entry into the job market. The primary quality employers look for in an unskilled position is reliability, and most report that the best way to find reliable employees is by personal referral. Where a group like Hope Now For Youth did the screening of referrals, employers were willing to "take a chance" on people they normally would not have hired because they trusted the judgment of the director, whom they knew – another example of the value of networks. The only job Lee ever got was through a friend who recommended him. Hope Now can and, by God's grace, will become Lee's network to a job.

We work one at a time, and can be discouraged either one

at a time or by the whole. Let these words of a 20<sup>th</sup> century champion of the poor be your encouragement.

## Mother Theresa Writes

I never look at the masses as my responsibility,
I look at the individual.
  I can love only one person at a time.
I can feed only one person at a time.
  Just one, one, one.
You get closer to Christ by coming closer to each other.
As Christ said,
  Whatever you do to the least of these my brethren
    you do to me - so you begin - I begin.
I picked up one person.
  Maybe if I didn't pick up that one person,
  I wouldn't have picked up 42,000.
The whole work is only a drop in the ocean,
    but if I didn't put the drop in,
  the ocean would be one drop less.
Same thing for you,
  same thing in your family,
    same thing in the church where you go.
      Just begin – one - one.
At the end of life we will not be judged by
  how many diplomas we have received,
  how much money we have made,
  how many great things we have done.
We will be judged by:
    I was hungry and you gave me to eat,
    I was naked and you clothed me,
    I was homeless and you took me in.
Hungry not only for bread, but hungry for love.
  Naked not only for clothing,
  but naked of human dignity and respect.
Homeless not only for want of a room of bricks,
  but homeless because of rejection.
This is Christ in distressing disguise.

My challenge to you this day is
    just begin - with one – one – one;
        begin today – with one – one – one.

Hok was Hope Now youth number one, the first youth we placed in a job, and he still is successful today as a Plant Utility Engineer at Children's Hospital Central California. God has been so good to us. Like Mother Theresa, we began with helping one, and that one youth has married the mother of his children and has bought a home. When I am downhearted, I think of Hope Now No. 1.

Souk could have been one of our early successes, but he broke our hearts by quitting a job to return to his crack addiction, and bolting from the in-patient care we suggested. In jail on Christmas Day, 1993, he penned this poem.

## I'M LYING IN HERE

I'm lying in here. My life tonight:
Unable to sleep, my mind runs riot.
I just review memories from the past,
Wondering why time's gone so fast.

I think of the days I was a bad child,
Just a carefree guy running totally wild.
My thoughts of the future were often shattered
By things of the present that didn't matter.

When I grew older, my ways were the same.
I had the idea that life was a game.
So to win I cheated, but instead I lost,
And now I'm the loser paying the cost.

Yet as I ponder these thoughts tonight,
I begin to see my past wasn't right.
I plan for a future that will keep me free,
So I better help myself before eternity.

Still, we did him some good. Christ loved him through us. Last we heard, in 1994, Souk had held a job for one month in Minnesota.

Six months before we began Hope Now For Youth, I found this poem written by one of the founders of Alcoholics Anonymous, an Episcopal priest. It beautifully portrays your mission and mine, the redeeming work of every sincere Christian. Here is the work of Hope Now.

## I STAND BY THE DOOR
### An Apologia for my life
by
Samuel Moor Shoemaker

I stand by the door.
I neither go too far in, nor stay too far out.
The door is the most important door in the world.
It is the door through which people walk when they find God.
There's no use my going way inside, and staying there,
     when so many are still outside,
And they, as much as I, crave to know where the door is.
And all that so many ever find
Is only the wall where a door ought to be.
They creep along the wall like blind people,
With outstretched, groping hands.
Feeling for a door, knowing there must be a door,
Yet they never find it.
So I stand by the door.
The most tremendous thing in the world
Is for people to find that door, the door to God.
The most important thing anyone can do
Is to take hold of one of those blind, groping hands
And put it on the latch, the latch that only clicks
And opens to that one's own touch.
Men and women die outside that door, as starving
     beggars die
On cold nights in cruel cities in the dead of winter —
Die for want of what is within their grasp.
Nothing else matters compared to helping them find it,
And open it, and walk in, and find Him.
So I stand by the door.

Jesus calls himself the Door. But he may appear in other guise to the oppressed. Mahatma Gandhi expressed it this way, "There are people in the world so hungry, that God cannot appear to them except in the form of bread." Set adrift by abandonment, rejected and abused youth first tie up to God at the moorings of a listening counselor, and Jesus smiles. There are gang members so desperate for employment that Jesus first appears to them as a job. And he is delighted to do so. Jesus is the Door, but he doesn't mind using squeaky hinges or a noisy knocker to point the Way.

Our spiritual hope for each man is that he gives his heart to the eternal joy and service of Christ. But we celebrate success if he keeps his job and stays away from crime and violence. There is joy in seeing him marry the mother of his children or purchase a home for his family. He may not now give thanks to the Savior, but he will never forget that walking into a church of Jesus Christ completely changed his life. When a grateful Thongkham was asked to speak at our annual banquet, he thought about it for a week, and then replied, "I owe it to Hope Now and to the men who come after me." Thongkham was remarkably articulate from a grateful heart. Unfortunately, however, forgetting to be grateful to Jesus seems to be a more common experience for youth helped by Hope Now. This ingratitude reminded me of Luke 17:11-19, which I applied to gang members.

## GIVING THANKS TO JESUS

As Jesus continued on into Fresno, he came to Kings Canyon Boulevard. As he went into a neighborhood there, ten gang members recognized him from a distance and cried out, "Jesus, Son of God, have mercy on us and our families! We want to earn money the right way but no one will hire us."

He looked at them and said, "Go to my servants at Hope Now and do what they say." And when these gang members listened to the counselors at Hope Now and did what was right, they were given jobs. One of them, when he saw that he had his first real job, came back to Jesus, shouting, "Praise

God, I no longer have to earn a living on the streets. I have a job!" He fell face down on the ground at Jesus' feet, thanking him for what he had done. Now this man had been a gang leader.

Jesus asked, "Didn't I give hope and jobs to ten men? Where are the other nine? Does only this gang leader return to give thanks to God?" And Jesus said to the man, "Stand up and go. Your faith has made you whole."

Whether they experience gratitude now, or not until later, looking down the corridors of time, many will be your sons and daughters in glory. Paul has never spoken to us about his mother or father. He was first incarcerated at age 13, and by age 19 he had spent almost one third of his life behind bars. Trust was a major issue with Paul; he couldn't figure out why we were helping him, even when we told him about Jesus. Suspicions and fears from a violent past haunted his thoughts by day and his dreams at night. "Why did the counselor help me get my birth certificate? Why did he help me get my driver's license? What does he want from me?" he wondered. We just wanted him to succeed at his job. When his counselor invited him to attend church, Paul brought his girlfriend and afterwards took his counselor out to lunch. What a beautiful act of thanksgiving!

Many will give thanks to God for you because of the wonderful grace God has shown through you. In 1997 our mayor said that what finally convinced Gap Clothing to base its Pacific Region Warehouse in Fresno was our city's precipitous drop in crime. We'd like to believe that Hope Now had a part in the Gap Clothing warehouse being located in Fresno, and when a person gives thanks for obtaining one of the 300 jobs there, he or she is thanking God for Hope Now as well. There's that iceberg phenomenon again – you'll never know all the good you're doing until we stand together before our Lord.

When a fight broke out during a Thanksgiving Dinner held for gang members at a church in 1993, an angry Vanna left with his friends to get a gun. They returned and did a driveby shooting, spraying bullets into the parking lot. The next day, when he read the newspaper report of one youth killed, Vanna knew he was wanted for murder. He ran but eventually turned himself in to the police. While jailed he read in the newspaper about a new organization started in 1993 to help gang members get a job, and thought, *"Where was Hope Now For Youth when I needed them in 1992?"* The jail chaplain gave him a book about tough criminals changed by Jesus and, after reading it, Vanna gave his heart to the Lord. For his crime, Vanna spent the next eight years in the California Youth Authority. While incarcerated, he listened to Christian radio programs, read Christian books from the chaplain's library, and was discipled by other inmates. When Vanna got out in 2001, he didn't believe Hope Now was still in existence. We give all glory to God that Hope Now was there to encourage him and get him a job as a church custodian for the city's largest congregation, Peoples Church. Working the swing shift allows Vanna to go to school during the day, becoming the first one in his family to attend college. How many gang young men in *your* city are searching in vain for a glimmer of hope? How many are groping along the wall, searching for the Door?

Hope Now believes that God is fulfilling his promise: *"They shall be called oaks of righteousness, a planting of the Lord, for the display of his splendor."* (Isaiah 61:3) So we continue to strive for excellence, and invite you to join us. *Excellence is the result of caring more than others think is wise, risking more than others think is safe, dreaming more than others think is practical and expecting more than others think is possible.* With the God and Father of our Lord Jesus Christ, truly all things are possible. Together then let us present this glorious Lord a thank offering of 1,000,000 ex-gang members lifted from 100,000 streets of 10,000 neighborhoods in 1,000 cities of America. Be assured that Jesus will never forget our grateful service. *"No eye has seen, no ear has heard, and no mind has imagined what God has prepared for those who love him"* (I Corinthians 2:9).